Anna Fuller

One of the Pilgrims

A Bank Story

Anna Fuller

One of the Pilgrims
A Bank Story

ISBN/EAN: 9783337106522

Printed in Europe, USA, Canada, Australia, Japan

Cover: Foto ©ninafisch / pixelio.de

More available books at **www.hansebooks.com**

One of the Pilgrims ✠ | A Bank Story ✠

By

Anna Fuller

———

G. P. Putnam's Sons
New York and London
The Knickerbocker Press
1898

Copyright, 1898
BY
G. P. PUTNAM'S SONS
Entered at Stationers' Hall, London

The Knickerbocker Press, New York

TO

R. F.

CONTENTS.

CHAPTER	PAGE
I.—The Pilgrims	1
II.—An Awkward Alternative	14
III.—The Widow O'Toole's Diplomacy	28
IV.—A Formal Introduction	42
V.—An Unambitious Hero	55
VI.—Miss Vickery at Home	68
VII.—High and Low	84
VIII.—A Pleasant Dinner	101
IX.—Flynn's Eyrie	118
X.—A Phenomenal Cure	132
XI.—Theory and Practice	144
XII.—Truxton's Utopia	157
XIII.—An Unlucky Windfall	170
XIV.—Forest Ways	185
XV.—A Good Shot	205

CHAPTER	PAGE
XVI.—Out of a Clear Sky	221
XVII.—Under a Cloud	236
XVIII.—Poor Everybody	252
XIX.—Flynn's Romance by Adoption	269
XX.—Humble Hospitalities	282
XXI.—The Tale of an Old Coat	296
XXII.—The Prose of It	309
XXIII.—The Poetry of It	323

One of the Pilgrims
A Bank Story

ONE OF THE PILGRIMS

CHAPTER I.

THE PILGRIMS.

"FLYNN, how old are you?" asked Frank Truxton, a junior clerk of the Pilgrim Savings Bank, one quiet morning in February.

It was what was known at the Pilgrim as the season of heavenly rest, when, if ever, social amenities are in order. Money was not to go on interest, neither was interest to fall due, for two months to come, and an air of elegant leisure pervaded the establishment, rather accentuated than otherwise by the occasional straggler driven by monetary surplus or deficit to make unseasonable application at the long counter.

Flynn paused in the process of wetting the "spinges," the most arduous duty still devolving upon the old janitor in his pension days. The "spinge" in question was a diminutive one belonging to the stout and fastidious Mr. Wilkinson, and Flynn gave it a tentative squeeze before committing himself to a reply. The result being a just sufficient ooze of moisture, the which showed no reprehensible tendency to detach itself from the surface of the sponge, Flynn concluded that he was at liberty to consider the searching question put to him. He turned his seamed and seared old face to his interlocutor and gave a transparently crafty glance at the quizzical eyes that met his. Then, with the rising inflection habitual to him, he said : " Fiftee, sixtee, siventee, wan, two, three,—somewhere along there, maybe."

It was always a shock to the uninitiated to hear Flynn speak. His dress was so much that of the modest, self-respecting gentleman, the silk hat which he wore on his humblest errands was so carefully brushed, his boots so neatly blacked, that his broad Irish brogue took the stranger by surprise. In his latter days, especially, when the savings of forty thrifty years had placed him in easy, not to say opulent, circumstances, when his semi-retirement on a pension had relieved him from the inconsiderable stress and strain of active service, his deportment had taken on an air of leisurely decorum by virtue of which he might easily have passed muster as a director of the bank. The gift for keeping his own counsel, so aptly illustrated in his reply to Truxton's question, had always characterized him.

"Here, here, Flynn," Truxton remonstrated with great apparent seriousness, "you're making yourself out nearly two hundred years old!"

"How's that, now?"

"Why, fifty and sixty and seventy are one hundred and eighty, to begin with, and one, two, three,—that's six more!"

The old man bestowed upon his ingenious inquisitor the look of supreme contempt which he always took refuge in when he found himself cornered, and saying, "That'll do, that'll do!" in the tone he might have adopted toward an importunate child, he turned on his heel and sauntered off to the rear. Here he established himself behind the morning paper and fell to speculating as to the probable meaning of certain three- and four-syllabled words which had intruded themselves into the account of so simple a matter as a recent burglary. For it should be borne in mind that English was a foreign tongue to Flynn, and, as Frank Truxton often took occasion to remark, the rest of the gang might bless their stars if they could speak any foreign tongue whatever as intelligibly as Flynn spoke English.

Flynn knew his value, and was never lavish with his society. The clerks might, in a moment of irritation, when he had fetched the wrong ledger or upset an ink-bottle, question whether he was more of a nuisance or an assistance to his fellow-workers; but we may be sure that no such doubt ever crossed his mind. Nor was he more convinced of his importance as one of the oldest props of the great Savings Institution than of the worth of his social qualities. He was perfectly well aware that he was not only a source of amusement but of perplexity to "thim young fellers"; that not one of them had ever quite made him out. As long as they did not know whether he meant to be funny or not, the salt of his casual remarks or his humorous protests would not lose its savor; and it was not in Barney Flynn's scheme to enlighten them on that head. Yes; they would miss "the ould man" when the "fiftee, sixtee, siventee" had ended in zero; they would that! Indeed, so keen was his sense of the void his departure would make, that he was half inclined to approve Andy Stone's somewhat startling proposition that when Flynn died they should have him stuffed and set in a corner, with the *Morning Trumpeter* in his hand. His own figure, thus piously preserved, sometimes presented itself to his imagination as he sat in his accustomed corner behind the newspaper, momentarily worsted, perhaps, in his encounter with the long words, and he had a very strong impression that that stuffed figure would be the chosen haunt, during bank hours at least, of his otherwise disembodied spirit. Certainly he would be loath to relinquish his guardianship of the institution so long as "that good man, Misther Trooxton," continued to enliven its austere precincts with his cheerful presence.

Flynn had already served close upon forty years in his capacity of Guardian Angel to the Pilgrim Savings Bank—a function erroneously defined as janitor on the pay-roll of the institution—when young Truxton made his appearance in the ranks some two years since.

"Wal now!" he had declared, with a falling inflection, in answer to the new clerk's inquiries,—and it may be well to note at the outset that Flynn's inflections were in most cases precisely the reverse of those which would be selected by an Anglo-Saxon in a similar instance;—"Wal now! me and Barry was the furst wans here of this gang. Saymar, he coom along a matther of six years afther."

The gentleman thus lightly designated was none other than Mr. Rufus Seymour, the treasurer of the institution, a dignitary for whom Flynn, in his heart of hearts, entertained a more profound respect than for any other human creature outside St. Peter's chair. But Flynn liked to have his little fling in the presence of a green hand, and this bit of bravado had for him something of the same fearsome relish that the piously brought-up youth finds in his initial ventures in profanity. Who can say, too, that the old man may not have had a sly notion of testing the quality of his new colleague? One never knew whether or not to read between the lines of Flynn's remarks; that was one secret of his fascination. Whatever may have been his motive, it is easy to imagine the glow of pleasure with which he listened to the youngster's grave rejoinder.

"Really," Truxton had observed; "you 've kept Seymour on for quite a while. He has given good satisfaction, I take it."

"Pretty fair, pretty fair," Flynn admitted, with a shrug of the shoulders, and an indescribable grimace, intended to express a deprecatory indulgence. "The man manes well, he do that!"

From that day forth, Flynn was the sworn friend and ally of young Truxton, whom Harvey Winch promptly christened "Flynn's protejay." Not that the young man was in any particular need of an ally and patron. On the contrary, he had early scored almost as marked a success with his fellow-clerks as with the admiring Flynn, and his popularity showed as yet no signs of waning. He was possessed of a number of qualities which are calculated to ensure the good-will of one's fellow-creatures.

To begin with, there was his sense of humor, a gift of primary importance in any walk of life which brings a man in contact with that order of human beings which, in a democracy, may perhaps be most acceptably designated as the exasperating classes. The term high and low may be very properly eliminated from the vocabulary of the consistent republican, but it will be long before the mere principle and practice of democracy will eliminate from the composition of a sovereign people that density as to money transactions which characterizes Pat and Beppo and even Hiram, together with their respective women-folk, more obviously, if not more essentially, than those who have enjoyed greater educational advantages.

Truxton was not a wit; he was hardly what our grandfathers would have termed a wag. That post was filled by Aleck Plummer, the paying-teller, a keen, sometimes caustic, commentator on life, a man of brains, to boot, and of real financial ability. Yet to Truxton, who rarely made a brilliant sally, and never a cutting one, was given the faculty of discovering in the most trying situation, in the most gratuitously aggravating depositor, that delicate, often illusive, grain of humor which, to him who has the perception to find it, is the saving salt of the most unpalatable dish. And not only had he an unerring sense of humor, but he was also possessed of the gift of mimicry, by means of which he could pass on his impressions to less favored ones.

There was James Judson, for instance, the elderly accountant, confessedly so deficient in humor that he was capable of conversing for fifteen minutes on end with Bridget Ballahak, the bank's favorite depositor, without experiencing any other sensation than one of helpless annoyance. Yet the sober-minded Judson had been known to laugh audibly at Truxton's impersonation of Lydia

Lally, a buxom and enthusiastic widow of the down-east persuasion, whose tone had become unduly confidential under the influence of the younger clerk's amused sympathy. And this, although the open-hearted Lydia was a depositor of ten years' standing, whom nobody had " discovered " prior to the advent of Truxton, while the redoubtable Bridget was a lady, the first glimpse of whose phenomenal bonnet was exciting to the risibles, and whose riotous eloquence had once caused little Billy Denison to tumble over the waste-paper basket, from sheer inability to hold himself upright. There could be no question of the social supremacy of a man who could make James Judson laugh audibly over the down-east widow.

But although Truxton could get much innocent mirth for himself and his fellow-pilgrims out of the unconscious depositors, who were not only none the worse for it, but were thereby rendered interesting and acceptable members of society, he was rarely, if ever, guilty of an indiscretion where his friends were concerned. If the corpulent Wilkinson was sensitive as to his weight, he need not dread being reminded of it by Frank Truxton; if Harvey Winch, who prided himself upon his rather shaky French, was familiarly known by the name of Polly Voo, he was well aware that he did not owe the obnoxious sobriquet to the genial humorist whose desk was next his own. Even George Bodley, who was everybody's butt, mainly because he was so good-natured that nobody was afraid of him, even he had not yet been made to wince by any word or act of Frank Truxton's. And this tactfulness on the part of the young man was so manifestly due to his being a thoroughly good fellow, that it was doubly endearing to those who profited by it.

When one adds to these mental and moral attributes an open and prepossessing countenance, and a certain ease and force of bearing which made itself felt in the very way his head was set on his shoulders, it becomes apparent that Flynn was not far wrong in opining that " next to mesilf an' Misther Saymar that young Trooxton is about the best man o' the lot ! "

Truxton was the youngest but one of the pilgrims—as the clerks were wont to style themselves—being now just turned twenty-seven, and when, a few months since, it leaked out that he was dabbling in Colorado mining-stocks, an interest and concern little short of grandfatherly manifested itself among the men. And it was at this juncture that the discovery was made that Truxton, with all his good-nature, could, when he chose, be as reticent as the best of them. Yes, he rather guessed there was gold in Colorado; it could hardly be all a fake. No, there was no particular mine that he had special confidence in. It was pretty much all a gamble, anyway. The general impression seemed to be that the cheap stocks offered the best chance for a rise. He had a friend out there, a stock-broker. Would anybody like his address?

There was something about his bearing in such interviews that forbade categorical questions, and by the time three of his friends had said enough to convince a youth of less ready perceptions that they were, one and all, eager to ruin themselves in stock-gambling, the conviction had struck root among them that Truxton proposed to mind his own business, and expected other people to mind theirs. As his spirits were unflagging, however, and his attention to business as prompt and satisfactory as usual, his friends embraced the hope that a merciful fate had visited upon him at the outset a precautionary experience of ill-luck, thereby saving him from serious disaster. No one knew what Truxton's pecuniary resources might be, but it was safe to conclude that a man in opulent circumstances would not elect to handle small bills at a moderate salary.

Meanwhile their minds had taken another turn, thanks to the initiative of the astute Flynn. For it is a fallacy entertained by women, literary persons, tramps, and that ilk, instilled into their too receptive minds by those who ought to know better, that business is business and nothing else. If business is the occupation which men pursue in the haunts of trade and finance, it is much besides business. It is observation and inference on many other subjects than dollars and cents; it is interest in one's fellow-creatures, their traits and foibles, their fortunes and misfortunes. And a man who could spend five or six hours of every day in the uninterrupted contemplation of dollars and cents, or their inky symbols, would be a monster of inhumanity such as, luckily, has never yet found its way into the ranks of the good old Pilgrim.

It was therefore not without a certain pleasant assurance as to the reception his hint was likely to meet with, that Flynn had sidled up to Rathbone, the receiving-teller, one busy day, a few weeks previous, and remarked, in a stage whisper which only seemed to accentuate the brogue of it: " Sure, an' it 's a nate figger she has on her! "

Rathbone took time to request " Dinnis O'Flannigan, your Honor " to assort the miscellaneous collection of small bills to the amount of " siventy-wan dollars " with which that Hibernian capitalist was desirous of enriching the coffers of the bank, and graciously to accept two silver dollars which a puny, fourth-rate housemaid proffered, before he glanced in the direction indicated by Flynn.

Taking her leave of Truxton with a nod and a smile of unmistakable good understanding, was a very charming and charmingly clad young woman with the " natest " kind of a " figger on her." Rathbone knew her well by name and face. For several years past she had been a frequent visitor at the bank, having in charge the accounts of a number of Irish and Italians, on whose books she was in the habit of making small deposits from time to time.

Rathbone, who was rather fond of taking the unpopular side in questions of the day, and who professed a hardened scepticism in regard to philanthropic works—though it must be admitted that the trained instinct of the professional beggar had long since pierced this shallow pretence,—Rathbone, the sceptic, had opined that it was a crying shame for a girl like that to bother her head about those good-for-nothing paupers. Your professional sceptic, by the way, is nothing if not illogical, and, for argumentative purposes, a savings-bank capitalist was as good a pauper as another.

On the occasion of Flynn's stage whisper, the receiving-teller had the satisfaction of assuring himself that Miss Ruth Ware was not so exclusively given over to good works as to be oblivious to the pleasanter aspects of life, the which, in this instance, were fairly well represented in the person of Frank Truxton.

And since there exists a wide-spread impression that business men, even if not the sticks and stones which they are popularly represented as being, are at least above gossip, it is impossible for the present chronicler to offer any good working theory in explanation of the fact that the next time Miss Ruth Ware had occasion, in the transaction of her business, to exchange a word with Truxton, more than one of the clerks was as keenly aware of the fact as Barney Flynn himself.

It was the morning of that philosopher's carefully considered response to Truxton's indiscreet inquiry as to his age, he being still withdrawn behind his newspaper fastness, that he became aware that she was "by." He peered out from behind his paper, taking in not only the attractive young woman and her interlocutor, but the little breath of interest, imperceptible to the uninitiated, which just stirred the gang on that quiet February morning, and, when the young lady stepped lightly away, Truxton, reluctantly turning his eyes from her retreating figure, heard a voice at his elbow remarking, in a tone of the most insinuating intelligence: "Howly Mary! but how spry she is on her feet!"

That was all,—but one glance at the face at his shoulder, with its look of abnormal sagacity, was enough. Truxton knew that he was betrayed.

CHAPTER II.

AN AWKWARD ALTERNATIVE.

NOT that there was anything in particular to betray when all is told. If the beginning of Frank Truxton's acquaintance with Miss Ruth Ware had been marked by certain unusual features which gave it a character of its own, it had not yet progressed so far as to claim the attention of the curious. In order, therefore, to do justice to a situation in which the genial Flynn had created a factitious interest, it is necessary to recur to the circumstances of a certain introduction which had taken place some few weeks previous.

And, first of all, since introductions are in order, it should be stated that Miss Ruth Ware was a young woman of some little consequence in what is technically known as society, a consequence which she owed primarily to the fact that her family had for several generations been people of character and means. She was, however, of at least equal consequence in an humble world of her own choosing, where neither character nor means was conspicuous, and this importance was a much more individual affair, being due to strictly personal considerations.

If any other child of Mr. Caleb Ware's had gone in for philanthropy he would have deprecated the step—and deprecation on Mr. Ware's part was a pretty serious matter for his family—but to Ruth he offered no opposition. This was partly because she made so little stir about her good works that it was quite possible for her people to forget what her elder brother designated as her " extensive acquaintance among our foreign constituency," and partly because of her father's well-founded conviction that she was too levelheaded to run things into the ground.

Ruth Ware, then, thanks to the possession of a fair degree of good judgment and an engaging personality, had made herself morally the prop and mainstay of more than one tottering edifice of family life. She had even, in a number of instances, succeeded in establishing a solid underpinning of thrift and self-respect, more enduring than any outside support.

Among other qualifications for her chosen task, she possessed a quite unusual faculty of extracting, from a seemingly depleted exchequer, stray coins which might otherwise have filtered away into the sand of hereditary wastefulness or hereditary worse-than-that, and no lingering and wistful glances of Lucia, no deprecatory growls of Pat, could move her to abate one jot of her exactions. As a consequence of this firm and sagacious policy, it had more than once occurred that the improvident Pat had waked one fine morning to find himself a capitalist to the tune of some thirty-odd dollars in the Pilgrim Savings Bank ; or that the inconsequent Lucia had imbibed, in a misty way, the knowledge that a hundred ten-cent pieces entrusted to this remarkable financial hot-house were productive, in course of time, of other ten-cent pieces of equally authentic coinage. This was, of course, something far beyond the mental grasp of the beautiful and appealing daughter of Italy ; but then, was not the world a storehouse of mystery, and why should not the same great Power that had snatched her baby from her, and had closed her ears so that she could not comprehend the human speech of this strange land, perform, just once in a way, a small miracle in behalf of *la poverina ?*

It is not to be inferred that our financiering philanthropist bore to the bank each dime and quarter fresh from the reluctant hand of its owner. On the contrary, she rarely offered for acceptance a deposit of less magnitude than five dollars, and the private banking business which she was thus obliged to carry on in her own purse, so to speak, involved her in an endless task of bookkeeping, the performance of which would have done credit to James Judson, or the Secretary of the United States Treasury. This somewhat incongruous association of ideas, by the way, may find its justification in Aleck Plummer's confident assertion that there is quite as much brain-work required in the calculation of nickels as in that of millions, and that, as far as the larger question of surplus and deficit goes, the problem which the United States Treasurer, with all his vast resources, has to solve, is a mere bagatelle when compared with that of a man whose income is insufficient.

Be that as it may, Ruth Ware performed her own modest task with gratifying success, and as often as one of her open accounts approached the five-dollar limit she gloated over it with a satisfaction little short of avaricious.

So enamored was she of the Pilgrim Savings Bank and its beneficent mission in the world, that she had once ventured so far out of her accustomed line of influence as to advise Ophelia Pye, a young Vermont seamstress of her acquaintance, to deposit there the whole of a seven-hundred dollar legacy which had recently dropped like a sudden sunbeam into the meagre, toilsome life of the girl. Ophelia, who had an unbounded respect for Miss Ruth's judgment, reinforced in this instance by her own native New England thriftiness, repaired forthwith to the Pilgrim Savings Bank, where she already had a small account, there to deposit her treasure.

It was quarter-day and a long line of people were waiting their turn. She took her place in the queue and resigned herself to the slow progress of events. Very slow it was, too, but like all but the classic lane it had its turning, and at the end of twenty minutes she found herself only two removes from the counter. She opened her book, between the leaves of which she had placed her roll of bills. The money was gone!

For a hideous moment the poor girl's heart stopped beating; then it made up for lost time, and her brain labored with equal rapidity. She instantly remembered that she had not examined her book since leaving home; she remembered also having handled it rather carelessly in making room for a neighbor on the seat of the car in which she had come down town. So clear was she that she had then and there dropped the money, that she turned without a word of inquiry and left the bank.

The line closed in behind the spare young figure, as the stream of life always closes in upon a gap, and one by one, in slow, almost rhythmic, succession, the other drops of the stream detached themselves and trickled off in their widely diverging channels. Yet not until the clocks of the city struck two, and Flynn, standing stern as Fate with his hand upon the great door, closed it against belated comers, did the stream show signs of diminution. It was close upon three o'clock before the current had fairly spent itself and the tired clerks could take time to breathe.

The last depositor of all had been a giddily

dressed, well-to-do Irish woman who gave her name as Catharine Murphy. She was a new depositor, and Rathbone, knowing well the propensity of the average man and woman to withhold a possible middle name until some later day, when the inconsiderate announcement of it cannot fail to confuse the counsels of the bookkeeper, was subjecting her to a searching inquiry on that head.

"Have you a middle name?" he had asked in the prompt business tone which brooks no evasion.

"What's that, sorr?"

"Have you a middle name?"

"Is it a middle name your honor was afther axin'?"

"Yes: have you a middle name?"

The careful enunciation of the sentence was equalled only by the simplicity of its tenor.

"Wa-al," said Catharine, making several syllables of the word, and contracting her features in a speculative scowl, "whin I was a gyurl in the——"

"*Have you a middle name?*" Rathbone thundered, in so fierce and blood-curdling a voice that all the clerks paused delightedly to listen, while Flynn edged a trifle nearer.

The dressy depositor, frightened almost out of her wits, gathered herself together for a desperate effort and with shaking voice replied, "Naw, sorr; I'm a widdy lady!"

The rest of her business was transacted under a cloud of irritation on the one side and of agitated anxiety on the other, and the widow lady was only too glad to make good her escape through the door which Flynn held open for her, in a gingerly manner, as if expecting countless hordes to storm the fortress.

Flynn, whose labors were thus brought to a close, turned away from the door, a portentous frown upon his furrowed countenance. It had been an arduous day for the old janitor, whose function on such occasions was to keep the line in order ; an undertaking requiring the alertness of a shepherd dog when the flock is on its travels. He donned hat and coat with a weary air, and as he passed Truxton's desk he remarked, in a tone of profound discouragement : " These Irish women martifies me ! "

A couple of hours later, Truxton, who chanced to be one of the last to leave the bank, passed out from behind the counter. As he directed his steps toward the door he espied a small object lying in the shadow under a settee. Curiosity and fatigue had a short but sharp conflict in which the former triumphed and, stooping, the young man picked up what proved to be nothing less than Ophelia Pye's roll of bills. He was at a loss to understand how such a sum of money should not have been missed and reported, but this was happily no concern of his, and, handing the bills over to the paying-teller, who was still immersed in figures, he made his way to a neighboring café in search of a dish of chowder. He was very glad that the money had not been swept away with the waste papers, but he was still more immediately gratified to find that the chowder was hot and palatable.

A cautious advertisement was inserted in the daily papers, making so vague an allusion to a sum of money found in the city that it seemed doubtful whether it would attract the attention of the rightful owner, while it would have been a sanguine impostor indeed who should have attempted to gain unlawful possession of it.

Happily for Ophelia Pye, and happily, too, perhaps, for Miss Ruth Ware, the latter had been apprised of the disastrous outcome of the undertaking which she herself had instigated, and no item of the newspaper "Founds" was likely to escape her notice.

It was the January quarter, when interest does not fall due at the Pilgrim, and a lull had quickly succeeded the turmoil of the past week or two. Two days after quarter-day Truxton was sitting at his desk, which stood at some distance from the counter, when he became aware of a little eddy of interest centring about a certain point. Mr. Smith, the vice-treasurer, had come down from the front office, and was engaged in earnest conversation with two young women, one of whom was a familiar figure among the depositors. Truxton recognized her as that nice girl whom Rathbone liked to growl about because she was wasting herself on paupers. At the moment she was listening intently to the dialogue that was going on between her companion and the vice-treasurer, and somehow, as Truxton studied her unconscious countenance, it was borne in upon him that Rathbone's concern was probably gratuitous. The face was singularly sympathetic—there could be no doubt of that—but neither could there be any doubt of the humor and the good sense which were so refreshingly apparent in the cut of the eyes and the play of the features. He had a notion, too, that that bright warm brown hair was usually associated with a cheerful disposition. In short, he felt encouraged to believe that this young woman's philanthropic tendencies might be fruitful of as much good to others and as little harm to herself as is to be reasonably anticipated of any human enterprise.

On this occasion at least she had apparently succeeded in accomplishing her object, for Mr. Smith, after exchanging a few words with her, nodded his head with a look of grave conviction and, turning, gave an order to one of the clerks. There was much noting of details upon an official blank, a roll of bills was produced, a paper was signed by both young women, and Truxton thought, with a passing interest, that the $750 had found an owner.

He had made an addition that would not prove,

a circumstance not perhaps to be wondered at, and he was on the point of rectifying it when he heard a voice, close at hand, saying : " Truxton, you 're wanted. The owner of that money you found has turned up, and she wishes to thank you."

" Oh, the devil ! " Truxton exclaimed in lively perturbation. " I don't want to be thanked ! "

" I 'm afraid you can't get out of it," said Mr. Smith, much amused. " Step up and face the music like a man."

" I 'll be blessed if I won't pocket the next roll of bills I find," the victim protested, accepting the situation with the worst possible grace.

As Truxton approached the counter where the two young women were standing, he found himself wishing that it were the pretty one that he had to deal with. They would understand one another, he thought, with a word ; at least there would be no ridiculous fuss about it. But this pale, homely, ill-dressed one had a look of tragic tension about her which boded ill for the interview.

" This is Mr. Truxton," the vice-treasurer announced ; " the gentleman who found your money. Good day, good day ! "—upon which he considerately turned away, leaving Truxton unobserved in his discomfiture—unobserved by him, at least, but intensely conscious of a pair of pleasant brown eyes that were regarding him with a friendly interest almost as distasteful to him at that moment as the ardent though embarrassed gratitude of the poor seamstress.

"I wanted to thank you, sir, for my money; I am very grateful to you"; and with that the agitated Ophelia held out her hand in which Truxton beheld to his horror a ten-dollar bill.

"You misunderstand the thing," he protested, in real consternation. "The money was found here in the bank. I had no more choice about passing it in than if it had been handed me for deposit."

The pale, pinched face of the girl flushed slowly.

"It was all I had," she said, still proffering the obnoxious bank-note; "and you have saved it for me. You must let me thank you for it."

"I tell you I can't!" cried Truxton, sharply, about to turn his back upon a preposterous situation.

Ruth Ware was busying herself with the contents of a neat little embroidered bag which she held in her hand. She had perceived from the outset that Ophelia was blundering, but she could not well interpose. At Truxton's words she involuntarily looked up, struck by the harshness of the young man's tone and manner, which he himself was only half aware of.

But Ophelia could not yield. Her Yankee sense of the fitness of things made it morally impossible for her to pocket all that money without taking the only means known to her of acknowledging her obligation.

"Please take it!" she urged, and there was a

break in the voice that arrested the attention of the young man who was about retreating from the field.

He turned and saw that there were actual tears in the girl's eyes, and that the worn face looked hurt and grieved. He could not stand out against that. Better disgrace himself in a prosperous woman's sight than pain like that a poor and forlorn one.

"Very well," he said, extending his hand; "as you wish; and thank you very much."

Five minutes later he had looked up Ophelia Pye's address on the books and was writing a check for ten dollars to her order.

Ruth Ware, walking up the hill to the pleasant old elm-grown square where her father's house stood, wished that she could have been sure of the young man's motive in this sudden change of front. She liked to believe that he had sacrificed his pride to spare Ophelia's feelings—in fact, it was difficult for her not to believe it; but she was training herself not to take the foolishly optimistic view of her kind. And, perhaps because she was not able to satisfy herself on this head, she thought often that day of the young bank-clerk—of the pleasant character his face had preserved under the successive emotions of embarrassment, irritation, and—was it compunction? She hoped so. A man with just his particular turn of countenance must have nice perceptions. And very glad she was to find the supposition verified the following evening by the note which Ophelia came to advise with her about.

"For you see, Miss Ruth," Ophelia said, "I want to do what is right, and I think this money belongs to him; but I don't know how to make him take it."

The two young women were sitting together in the room that had been Ruth's ever since she could remember. It was a room with an atmosphere, thanks to which Ophelia seemed no more out of place in it than the mistress herself, though the latter chanced on this occasion to be making an unusually fine appearance. She was dressed for the opera; but Ophelia, quite oblivious of this accidental magnificence, had eyes only for the face from which she hoped to gather light and counsel.

Ruth took the note and read it with a glow of satisfaction. It ran as follows:

"MISS OPHELIA PYE,

"*Dear Madam:* It was most kind of you to offer me this generous gift, but I should be a rascal if I were to accept it. So please say no more about it. I am thankful that you have got your money back, and I hope you will hold on to it this time.

"Yours truly,
"FRANK TRUXTON."

"Well, Miss Ruth," Ophelia asked, "what do you advise me to do?"

Ruth looked up from the letter which she had twice read through.

"Do? Why, there's nothing to do. He is right and you are wrong."

"You really think so?"

"Of course I do."

"And hadn't I ought to have offered him the money?"

"I don't know whether you ought or not," said Ruth; "but I am very glad you did."

Hours later, when Ruth Ware sat again before her fire, burning low and dim, the thought of Ophelia's letter got itself caught in a wayward, reminiscent strain of music that the *Meistersänger* had left echoing through her brain. And it happened that, dismissing for a moment the melodious cobblers, she let herself be stirred once more by the memory of a certain homely incident of real life until, before she knew it, she found herself saying, under her breath: "That is what I call chivalrous!"

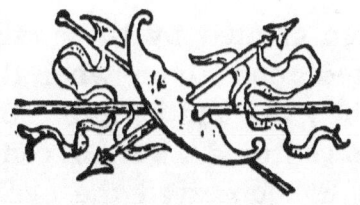

CHAPTER III.

THE WIDOW O'TOOLE'S DIPLOMACY.

AS for Frank Truxton, it was with anything but satisfaction that he thought of the incident from which Miss Ruth Ware was drawing inferences so complimentary to himself. He had been forced to do a particularly distasteful thing, to place himself in a false position in the eyes of a girl whose approval could not be indifferent to anybody—or so he told himself. Supposing he was nothing to her; supposing she would never think of him again,—and he devoutly hoped that might be the case,—it was nevertheless intolerable to have played the part of a cad in her eyes.

The irritation created by these reflections was promptly visited upon Flynn when that watchful guardian of the gang and its interests, individual and collective, ventured a word of congratulation. The old man had observed the encounter from afar, in no little anxiety lest Truxton should spurn the fairly earned reward, and so great was his relief at the outcome of the matter that he could not refrain from comment. He was also profoundly curious to learn the exact figure of the bill which had changed hands.

"Faith an' a hoonderd wad ha' been little enough in the primises," he remarked, airing a phrase which he had picked up out of the papers, and which he made tentative use of, from time to time, with a view to fixing its significance.

"Confound you, Flynn, what a donkey you are!" Truxton growled. "And look here; why in thunder don't you attend to your business, and have an eye out for the money people fling about on the floor? You passed that settee a dozen times before I did the other day, and you paid no more attention to that great wad of bills than if it had been an old boot-heel!"

Flynn's countenance assumed the look of philosophic tolerance which it always took on when he was found fault with.

"Aisy, aisy," he remonstrated, in a soothing tone. Then, with ill-suppressed curiosity, "Was it a dirty wan she was afther givin' yez—the mane-spirited crathur?"

"Look here! If you don't clear out of this, you'll see blue blazes!" cried Truxton, driven to the verge of exasperation; and, though the threat was indefinite, the manner of it was so alarming that the old man thought it well to retire from the field.

A few minutes later Flynn, having recovered

from his momentary discomfiture, was giving Andy Stone an eloquent account of his "protejay's" unprecedented lapse of temper.

"He was that mad wid me, he was, that the eyes of him blazed like a cat's eyes under the bed; an' I've seen it done, too!" he added, with a pardonable pride in this new evidence of the interest and variety of his experience of life.

When he passed Truxton's desk again, Flynn was booted and spurred for an important errand, being bound on a foraging expedition after sandwiches, doughnuts, and the like delicacies with which, in all but the busiest seasons, the gang could surreptitiously stay the pangs of hunger. Conscious of a grievance, he held himself very erect, and did not deign to cast a glance in the direction of his hot-headed young friend; but Truxton, bent on reconciliation, called out: "Here, Flynn; if you're going out, just drop this letter in the box, will you? And I say, Flynn,"—for the old man had taken the letter in cold silence—"have a cigar!"

That was an advance which Flynn could not withstand. He hated "thim onhatherly little tobakker sticks," and he would not have exchanged his good clay pipe for a box of Havanas; but nothing tickled his vanity more than to have one proffered in just that offhand, friendly manner, and Truxton knew it.

A glance at the address of the letter convinced Flynn that Truxton had been writing to the "gyurl." Not that he was scholar enough to decipher every chance superscription at a glance. But he had picked up the name of the girl, and it stood to reason that Ophelia must begin with an O, one of the few letters of the alphabet which no chirography can well disguise. He had no delicacy about imparting his information to such of the pilgrims as he was on confidential terms with, so that it was pretty well understood, before closing, that Truxton had sent back the money which he had surprised them all by accepting. A fortunate accident, indeed, since it did not occur to Truxton to offer any information on the subject. His course of action being the only one open to him, it would have struck him as quite unnecessary to state that he had taken it.

Had it not been for Miss Ruth Ware, the really trifling incident would have been promptly and finally dismissed from the mind of the chief actor in it. As it was, however, Truxton, for the first time in his life, found his equanimity at the mercy of one of his fellow-creatures. To his mortification, he was obliged to admit that he could not contemplate the possibility of a visit to the bank from that inoffensive young woman, without experiencing a distinctly uncomfortable sensation; and when, a week later, he was unexpectedly brought face to face with her in a new environment, his first impulse was to take ignominious refuge in flight.

Yet the two young people could hardly have

met under more favorable auspices than were accorded them by a friendly, one might almost say an ingeniously friendly, fate.

It happened that they were, all unawares, the fortunate possessors of a common friend, and it was to her that they owed what may be termed their social introduction. This was no other than the Widow O'Toole, an ex-laundress of the Ware family, an acquaintance whom Ruth valued highly, and whom she was in the habit of calling upon from time to time in her neat, semi-suburban tenement.

Now this neat tenement chanced to be the property of Miss Lucretia Vickery, the aged relative with whom Frank Truxton made his home, a lady of so much energy and independence of character that it had cost her a severe struggle when, some six months since, she had so far yielded to the infirmities of age as to relinquish to her grandnephew the collection of her rents. Miss Vickery herself lived not far from her own tenants, in a generous old square house, standing well back from the street, a house which still maintained something of its ancient dignity, situated though it was in a discredited neighborhood, and looking sadly in need of a new coat of paint and other details of its pristine toilet.

But although Miss Vickery held her head high, and never forgot that her father had sat in the national House of Representatives, she was also not without reminders that her present income was quite insufficient to support her legitimate pretensions. There is a certain dignity in the position of one who has met with reverses. The term conveys an assurance of possessions in the past, quite different from that implied in a statement that he has lost his money. In reverses there is no mercantile flavor, no suggestion of lucre lightly acquired and lightly lost; the plebeian image of money itself is quite excluded from consideration. And we may be very sure that Miss Vickery never, in her inmost thoughts, permitted herself to remember that it was actual dollars and cents that had been subtracted from her income, nor that the inconveniences of the situation had been due to such sordid causes as a drop in stocks in one quarter, or depreciated real estate in another; far less then, that she had been all but robbed by the family black sheep of a generation or two ago, a man whose good intentions could not save him from an incurable and disastrous tendency to speculate unsuccessfully. She had met with reverses—a misfortune peculiarly incident to gentle-folk—that was all; and the two dollars a week which she received from Margaret O'Toole, and a like sum derived at present with unexampled regularity from eleven other tenants of the Broad Street estate—this aggregate sum, minus taxes, water-rates, and repairs, constituted her entire income. To which should be added the contribution to the household expenses which her nephew made, and which each of them would have scorned to regard in the light of board-money.

The collection of weekly rents from a dozen more or less irresponsible tenants was no light task, and Miss Vickery was much impressed by the ease with which it was now accomplished. She had heretofore cherished a theory that the superiority of men to women in business matters was a groundless superstition; but when, week after week, her accounts came in, and she observed a cheering absence of those irregularities which had formerly disfigured them, she was constrained to bow to what must, after all, be an innate superiority of the masculine intellect. She never did things by halves, and once convinced that her nephew, who was little more than a stripling, could reduce the collection of rents to clock-like regularity, she was prepared to put the most favorable interpretation upon the acts of her butcher and her choreman, both of whom she had hitherto regarded as poor, inconsequent creatures, not to be trusted to their own guidance in the smallest particular.

Truxton's method had at least the advantage of simplicity. It consisted in advancing, out of his own purse, such small sums as were not forthcoming on the proper date, and he congratulated himself upon having hit upon so ingenious a device for sparing his aunt all possible annoyance. Once, indeed, he had been perilously near exposure.

It happened that the aforementioned Widow O'Toole had been inveigled into loaning a few dollars to a delinquent neighbor, and had failed to collect in time to meet her own obligations. For three successive weeks she had met Truxton with apologies and he, knowing her usual promptness, and disliking to press the good woman, had merely told her to take her time, having resort, on his own part, to his usual method of squaring accounts.

One fine morning, however, Mrs. O'Toole's neighbor paid up, as, indeed, the poor have a praiseworthy way of doing when dealing with their own kind, and the self-respecting O'Toole, having never before been backward with her rent, found herself quite unable to wait for payday to come round again. She accordingly arrayed herself in her brilliant-hued Paisley shawl, and her green kid gloves—No. 8—besides other choice features of a careful toilet, and, thus equipped, she hastened to her landlady's door, armed with her six dollars which she was prepared to proffer with many self-respecting apologies. The interview was a lively one, and Truxton will always regret that he was not privileged to participate in it.

Mrs. O'Toole found Miss Vickery seated in her high-backed chair in the long parlor, clad in her black Antwerp silk, a neatly darned crimson camel's-hair scarf across her shoulders, her snow-white hair partly hidden by a lace cap modelled upon one inherited from her mother. The exceptional elegance of her toilet was due to the fact that this was her reception day.

Ever since the family had returned, many years ago, from their sojourn in Washington, where the Squire's legislative honors had constrained them to reside, the Vickerys had been "at home" on Wednesday. One by one the inmates of the old house had slipped away to their final "at home" in the violet-strewn or snow-clad cemetery, and only Miss Lucretia was left to preserve the family tradition. One by one the neighbors, who had been used to observe with punctilious courtesy this declared preference on the part of Squire Vickery's family, had removed to a more fashionable place of residence inconveniently remote for social intercourse. Never yet, excepting during periods of mourning, had Miss Vickery failed to don her state gown and her pearl cross, to have the furnace heat all turned into the long parlor, and to establish herself in patient anticipation of the guest who so rarely came. By her side was a small claw-footed table on which rested her cut-glass bottle of lavender-water, her fan of marabou feathers and her photograph album; also a copy of N. P. Willis's *Poems*, which she was fond of committing to memory. She had once met Willis at a dinner in Washington, and his personal fascination had straightway gained for him the place in her heart of favorite poet.

Upon this tranquil scene, and into this dignified

presence, the Widow O'Toole was ushered on the memorable Wednesday afternoon on which Miss Vickery's newly acquired respect for masculine capacity was destined to be so narrowly jeopardized.

The visitor came in with a bobbing courtesy and a beaming face, and being very well aware that her call was not of a social nature she hastened to the consideration of business.

"Good-marnin' to yez, Miss Vickery," she began, standing in the middle of the room, as became her lowly station. "It 's mesilf as is ashamed to have been behind wid me rint owin' to a neighbor's man's father havin' fallen off the roof of a shed he was mendin' an' the family bein' called to lind a hand wid the ould man whin the coal was high and the eldest b'y out of a job an' the baby requirin' a fortin in Millin's Food. An' millins is no food says I for a young infant an' its not millins says she that I 'm afther givin' the child the way they grows out of the ground but the juice of 'em putt in a bottle I 'm thinkin' wid the seeds taken out an' a plaisin' taste o' milk an' pertaties mixed up wid it, an——"

Here Miss Vickery succeeded in stemming the torrent, a feat rendered the more difficult by the entire absence of punctuation in the widow's scheme of expression.

"But what is this you are saying about the rent, Mrs. O'Toole? Surely your rent has been paid up to date."

"Paid, is it?" cried the visitor, bridling perceptibly at this reflection upon her business intelligence. "Paid! An' me not knowin' it? An' is it a millionheiress ye 're takin' me for, to be payin' me rint unbeknownst?"

"You had better sit down, Mrs. O'Toole," the old lady commanded, conscious of an authority that was not to be gainsaid. "You seem to be tired and confused. Now let me explain to you," she added, soothingly, gratified by the promptness with which her visitor collapsed into the nearest chair. "Let me explain why I am so sure about it. My nephew reports to me each week, and he rendered his account on Monday, which shows all the rents in the Broad Street block paid up to date."

Miss Vickery had a habit of alluding to the "Broad Street block" in implied contradistinction to other pieces of property of an apocryphal nature.

To this assertion Mrs. O'Toole listened, open-mouthed.

"An' the Mike Talligans has paid, up to date?"

"Certainly."

"An' the Widow Dolan?"

"All the rents have been paid," the landlady asserted, with dignity. "Since my nephew undertook the management of the estate I have had very little trouble with my tenants. He brings to the task an executive ability and a business capacity which women are unhappily deficient in." Then, with a sudden consciousness that she was talking over her visitor's head, the speaker descended to a less abstract region of speculation. "Perhaps," she suggested, "you intended speaking to me on some other subject, and coming from the extreme cold outside, into this heated room,"—the thermometer in the long parlor had so signally failed to register more than sixty degrees in severe weather that it had long since been ejected from the premises,—"the sudden change in temperature has affected your memory. Do you not recall anything that you had meant to speak about?"

Now Margaret O'Toole was no fool, as she rarely lost an opportunity of declaring, and her processes of reasoning, though not profound, were swift. If the Talligans' rent was paid, if the Widow Dolan was not behind, and she out of work these three weeks, then it was "that honorable young gintleman that do be afther makin' it up to the ould lady." This deduction was as clear to her as print—clearer, indeed, since she had often assured Ruth that her "school-masther had died before she was born." It was not agreeable to suffer an imputation of mental derangement, but neither did it accord with her sense of propriety to betray "that swate young gintleman, the saints save him!" She hesitated a moment, and the mental struggle so clouded her usually alert countenance, still open-mouthed from the shock of surprise, that Miss Vickery was confirmed in her supposition.

"If you do not think of anything," the old lady said, kindly, "you had better step into the kitchen and let Bridget give you a cup of tea. It will warm you up for your walk home."

That settled it. A "sup o' tay" was a sovereign balm for a wounded spirit, and Mrs. O'Toole obediently pulled the long, red-tasselled bell-rope suspended from a small walking-beam arrangement under the ceiling, and meekly consigned herself to the guidance of Bridget, who appeared at the summons.

Miss Vickery would have been loath to admit, even to herself, the sense of exhilaration which this travesty of a call left in its wake. So few visitors came on her day, that even the Widow O'Toole counted for something.

Now this was the incident with which Mrs. O'Toole regaled Ruth Ware the next time that appreciative visitor came to see her, bringing, as a pretext, some embroideries to be done up.

The old woman was sitting in her big wooden rocking-chair, with a set of doilies, of sweet-pea design, spread over her neat calico person, while the pea-strewn centrepiece lay across Ruth's knees. The latter was listening with delighted interest to Margaret's account of how she had connived with the unconscious nephew in deceiving the old lady "wid the red scarf around hersilf." The picture was sketchy, but effective.

"Does Mr. Vickery know how quick you were?" Ruth asked; and a picture of a benevolent elderly capitalist presented itself to her imagination as candidate for the name she had so glibly pronounced.

"He doos that! It's himsilf as was afther sayin' that me talints was debloomatic in the quality."

"I am sure I think you behaved beautifully, Margaret, for you know you've got a temper of your own, and it was certainly very provoking at first."

"Timper, is it? Did ye iver see annybody from the County Tipperary that had n't a timper? Your honorable mother hersilf it was that says to me, says she, 'Margaret O'Toole, you'd better take your timper and trow it into the river,' says she, 'an' it's the best thing yez can do *wid it!*'"

The crinkles of delighted appreciation were deepening on the face of the listener, as she gave ear to this grotesque rendering of her "honorable mother's" admonitions, when, to her disappointment, the tale was cut short. A step resounded in the adjoining room, and, looking up at the intruder, Mrs. O'Toole cried: "It's himsilf come for the rint, an' me that can't move for the flowers on me like as if it was laid out for a wake I was!"

CHAPTER IV.

A FORMAL INTRODUCTION.

MRS. O'TOOLE, who was slightly deaf, had not heard Truxton's knock, while Ruth had been too preoccupied to heed it. Her delighted absorption in the old woman's narrative was only equalled by the orator's satisfaction in her own eloquence, and the announcement that "himsilf" was in the next room seemed to the visitor most inopportune.

Truxton had entered without much ceremony, knowing by past experience that if Mrs. O'Toole was not prepared to receive visitors the door would be locked and bolted. Only a week previous, in fact, he had been kept fully five minutes waiting for admission, a circumstance which, as Mrs. O'Toole had explained, was due to the fact that she had been trying a new way of doing her hair! The effort had evidently been prematurely interrupted, for she had finally made her appearance in a very tightly twisted pug, protruding from the southwest corner of her cranium, with a disregard for symmetry which betrayed a too hasty treatment.

On the present occasion Truxton had no sooner effected an entrance than he regretted his indiscretion; for he not only became aware that the mistress of the establishment was entertaining a visitor, but he instantly recognized his unconscious bugbear of the past fortnight. This, too, although Ruth was sitting with her back toward the door of the front room. There was no mistaking that shapely head, however, nor the hint of a profile furnished by the vanishing line of the cheek and the tip of a very individual nose.

The scene was a pretty one, and Truxton, with his habit of quick observation, took it in at a glance; the bright, bare kitchen with its overgrown cooking-stove, from every crevice of which a fiery red eye gleamed; the small window through which the sunshine streamed across a pot of rose-geranium; the two agreeably contrasting figures, leaning toward each other in reciprocal satisfaction. Despite the sunshine and the gleaming red eyes of the stove, despite the youthful coloring of her guest, it was the old woman herself, her brilliant cheeks and snapping black eyes, and the visible glow of eloquence on her emphatically speaking countenance which furnished the high-light of the picture.

Mrs. O'Toole had evidently made some recent progress in the difficult art of hair-dressing, for her animated head rejoiced to-day in a sort of irregular pyramid of doubtful composition, casually interspersed with strands of her own jet-black hair; a structure which created in the observer an anxious, almost painful interest, because of its manifest insecurity. The effect was heightened by a scarlet ribbon bow-knot, perched like a butterfly just below the apex of the pyramid, and which trembled sympathetically as often as its foundation tottered. It was clear that the widow had been making the most of the leisure secured to her by the monthly stipend of her son John's providing; and an ingrate this same John would have been, had he not treated his mother handsomely, for, as she never hesitated to declare, she had had "siven gyurls and wan b'y, an', beggin' your pardon, I set more store by the wan b'y than by all the gyurls put togither!"

The above, to be sure, is a digression, but a pardonable one, perhaps, considering the seductive nature of the subject. There was, about Margaret O'Toole's conversation, her conduct of life, her very personality, a certain diffuseness, a genial inconsequence, which may well impart itself to the methods of her too sympathetic portrayer. That lack of consecutiveness, if one may be allowed the expression, was well illustrated in the sharp contrast afforded between the pyramidal head-dress, the high color and shining eyes of the countenance on the one hand, and the severely decorous purple calico which composed the substructure of the piece.

A delicate foil to this highly flavored incongruity was furnished by the " nate figger " which Flynn was destined to observe and comment upon a few days later ; Miss Ware, on this occasion, being clad in a suit of dark-green serge, the harmonizing character of which, among the more brilliant tones of the picture, was pleasantly suggestive of the innate propriety observed by Nature in the choice of her predominant color. Both figures acquired a touch of picturesqueness, almost of poetry, through the lavish array of sweet-peas with which they were strewn.

In short, such an air of coziness and of genial sociability pervaded the scene that Truxton would have demurred at interrupting it even if there had been no bugbear to consider. As it was, he exclaimed, in a tone of deprecation bordering on alarm : " Please don't disturb yourself, Mrs. O'Toole ; I shall be round again this week, and there 's no hurry about the rent."

" Aisy, aisy, your Honor," Mrs. O'Toole cried, gathering up the doylies which seriously embarrassed her movements ; " it 's only Miss Ruth ! Miss Ruth, it 's himsilf ! "

Ruth, who had been lending a hand in harvesting the sweet-peas, could do no less than make her acknowledgments of so unmistakable a form of introduction, and, rising, she found herself face to face with Ophelia Pye's benefactor.

" Why, Mr. Truxton ! " she exclaimed, with undisguised pleasure ; " how many mutual friends we have! I think it's high time we were introduced!"

"It's very good of you to say so," said Truxton; "but I ought not to have come blundering in upon you. You were having such a pleasant time!"

"Take the gintleman into the parlor a minute, darlin'," Mrs. O'Toole was saying, "whiles I get out the rint. It's foine an' warm in there owin' to the foire in the stove blazin' up on me whin I was doin' up me hair an' me not mindin' to turn off the draughts till I 'd ha' been ash-fixurated like ould Jinny Maloney if I had n't suspicioned it was cooked I was gettin' an' throwed open the door on mesilf—so it's foine an' warm ye 'll find it, though it's divil a bit av sun do the room get whin it's naded, an' it's only in the scorchin' hot weather it pakes round the corner!"

With this purely perfunctory thrust at her landlady's representative, the old woman succeeded in driving her two guests out of the kitchen and closing the door upon them with much pushing of bolts and rattling of keys.

The situation was very absurd, and not a feature of it was lost upon either of the evicted guests, a fact which was apparent to each as they glanced at each other's faces.

"Nobody knows how long you will have to wait," Ruth said, with a shiver of amusement in her voice. "Margaret keeps her money buried forty fathoms deep — precisely where, I have never been able to find out."

"I always allow a quarter of an hour," Truxton admitted; "though I once knew her to produce a two-dollar bill in seven minutes and a half. Did you ever observe this work of art, Miss Ware?" He spoke in a craftily disengaged tone, as if the situation were the most natural in the world.

The work of art in question was a framed production, half chromo, half paper-doll, representing two simpering damsels, clinging devotedly to one another, and clad in actual tissue-paper skirts, the crude colors of which were somewhat softened by an opportune deposit of dust.

"It's a lovely thing," Ruth agreed, conscious of an unseemly desire to prolong the interview, which she the more promptly nipped in the bud. "But I am afraid I ought to be going. Margaret is so fascinating that I always find myself outstaying my time."

Now Ruth had imagined that, if she should ever have an opportunity of so doing, she should thank the young bank-clerk for his delicate consideration of Ophelia Pye's feelings. She had even wondered if it would not do to stop at the counter some day and speak about it. The moment she was brought into personal contact with him, however, she perceived that such a procedure was out of the question; that her intention implied an assumption of superiority on her part, as if, forsooth, it were for her to comment upon an act of simple good-breeding. When it came to the point, she would as soon have ventured to commend the young man for speaking grammatically or for removing his hat within doors. As she buttoned her jacket in pursuance of her intention to depart she was thinking how well she liked this new acquaintance, and what a pity it was that she might not stay a few minutes longer and have a talk with him.

Could Truxton have been aware of these ameliorating considerations, he would have been almost reconciled to her apparent eagerness to get away from him. He, too, would have liked a talk. It was very slow music standing about in this anything but royal antechamber, and it would not have been half bad to re-examine all its art-treasures in company with a girl who had so evident a relish for the inherent drollery of the O'Toole manifestation. What his thoughts were on the subject, however, or whether he had really detached his mind from the study of the pictorial paper-dolls, it was quite impossible to infer from the somewhat perfunctory tone in which he said: " I only hope I am not driving you away."

Ruth, meanwhile, had made a discovery.

" I don't think I shall drive myself away," she declared, in a tone of not too poignant regret, " if I can't make Margaret give me my fur cape. Margaret," she called, rapping sharply on the door, " Margaret, I've got to go home. Won't you please hand me my fur cape?"

A Formal Introduction 49

"Ach, be aisy, darlin'!" came the voice of the O'Toole, unnaturally muffled—could it be by the drawing of some garment over her head? "It's not a minute I'll be afther kapin' yez."

"But, Margaret, I've really got to go. Please hand me my cape through the crack of the door."

"An' would it be openin' the door ye'd have me, an' me wid me hair fallin' over me ears? It's himsilf as ud not know which way to look at all. Be aisy, darlin'. It's comin' I am in the turn o' your hand!"

"Well, hurry up," said Ruth; "and never mind your hair. Throw a shawl over your head and come along. There's really no special hurry," she added, turning once more to her companion in durance. "I only thought, if she began on that hair, it might detain us some hours, and I suppose we shall both be ready for our dinner sooner or later."

"*I* might go," Truxton suggested in a half-hearted manner; "I did n't wear my fur cape to-day!"

"Oh, please don't," Ruth cried. "I don't want to be left alone with those sentimental ladies in tissue-paper. It would be 'wurss again,' as Margaret would say."

"Good enough!" Truxton assented, with a sudden, absurd elation. "And why should we not pursue the study of art together?"

Now it is a very curious fact, and one which their biographer thinks worthy of mention, that this quite unexceptionable invitation to æsthetic delights struck both these young people as being surprisingly audacious and—agreeable. There are moments, as we all know, when the most commonplace word, the most trivial action, becomes significant ; and this does not necessarily occur at any given crisis, unless, indeed, the fact of its occurrence constitutes in itself a crisis.

"I suppose," Truxton remarked, as he directed his attention to a portrait of General Grant in full regimentals,—"I suppose we may consider that we now have the clue to the old lady's safety-deposit methods."

"I suppose we may," laughed Ruth. "In fact I have long had my suspicions. Have you never encountered an under-pocket among your depositors?"

"I blush to say I have," he admitted. "It seems to me one of the most striking developments of modern finance. It's curious," he added, transferring his attention to a plaster image richly arrayed in silk and spangles,—"it is curious, but there is always something sweet about the Madonna, no matter how they rig her out."

"Yes ; the sentiment never gets lost as it does with the poor saints. I suppose it is because it is something that everybody can understand. But," with a change of tone, "I'll thank you to speak more respectfully of this particular finery. That is a bit of one of my ball-dresses, I would have you to know."

It was a piece of pale-green silk, and it seemed to Truxton that it must have been becoming.

"Do you go in for that sort of thing?" he asked, trying to imagine her enacting the part of butterfly. Not very difficult either, on second thoughts. She was evidently not a girl of one idea.

"Not now," Ruth replied, serenely; "my day is past."

"Did you get tired of it?"

"Oh, no! I did n't have time; it got tired of me."

"I don't believe it," Truxton declared stoutly.

"You would if you were——" she hesitated, but not before he had caught her meaning.

"I doubt it," he replied, good-naturedly. "At any rate, if I *were*, I should try to make you change your mind."

"I only mean," said Ruth, thankful to him for helping her out of her difficulty,—"I only mean that we older girls don't get invited to balls, and so we naturally don't go."

"What a pity! Just as you are getting to be nicer than ever! I don't mean to be personal," he hastened to add.

"You don't? I flattered myself that you did!" and it suddenly struck Ruth that this was not her usual manner of talking to a stranger.

"Self-flattery is always a mistake," Truxton remarked, with mock sententiousness. "Flynn says—by the way, perhaps you don't know Flynn. He is the old ex-janitor at the bank."

"The one that dresses so genteelly, and takes such beautiful care of us on quarter-day? What has he got to say?"

"What has he not got to say, would be an easier question to answer. But perhaps my testimony ought to be ruled out, for Flynn vows that ' whativer thim fellers say I said, I say I did n't say it!'"

Whereupon Truxton found himself imparting to this most responsive of listeners one choice bit after another of Flynn's providing, while Ruth was beguiled into capping his stories with equally characteristic experiences of her own. And the outcome of it all was that this conversation, which did not again touch upon any personal theme, gave them an even clearer and more interesting impression of one another than of the ludicrous or pathetic specimens of humanity that formed their ostensible subject.

Ruth, for example, concluded that to be a bank-clerk—if only one possessed the creative touch—was to be something of a poet and very much of a dramatist. She found herself inclined to wonder that neither of her elder brothers, had embraced this remarkably fruitful calling, especially since her father happened to be a director of the bank in question. And then, even while she was laughing over Truxton's account of the Italian fruit-vendor whom the pilgrims could get rid of only by telling him that they had no money—thereby eliciting the excellent business axiom, "No money no banan's,"—even at that moment the thought crossed her mind that the pecuniary inducements of the situation might leave something to be desired. And then she recalled to mind the tale Margaret had told her of the old aunt "wid the red scarf round hersilf," and of the rents which she was never allowed to miss. So strong was the appreciative throb with which her imagination responded to these suggestions, that she hastened to make minute inquiries tending to identify the astute fruit-vendor with an acquaintance of her own in the same line of trade.

As for Truxton, he arrived at the conclusion, during those incalculable intervals which honeycomb the most animated conversation, that a pauper's lot was a very enviable lot indeed, some slight inconveniences and restrictions notwithstanding, if only it brought him in the way of ministrations from a certain quarter. It must furthermore be confessed that the sound of Margaret's voice at the door, heralding their release, was not the relief to either of these prisoners that it should properly have been.

"Are ye there, darlin'?" came the inquiry, while yet the door was hermetically sealed.

"Yes, Margaret; are n't you nearly ready to let us in?"

"An' is himsilf there?"

"Yes, Mrs. O'Toole; take your time, there 's no hurry!"—which daring assertion on the part of "himsilf" was not visited with the reproof which it merited.

There was a drawing of bolts and turning of keys, and Mrs. O'Toole appeared, wreathed in smiles, her hair dressed up to her latest model, and the red bow fluttering as nonchalantly on top as if it had never relinquished its perch.

"An' it's mesilf was afther tellin' yez I 'd be there in the turn o' me hand, an' it's as good as me wurrd I was. An' must ye be goin', darlin'?" for Ruth had hastily possessed herself of her cape and was waiting her chance to take leave. "It's sorry I am to lose the swate eyes of yez till ye come again, the saints save ye!"

Amid this and still further vociferous farewells, Ruth made good her escape, and, as she walked rapidly away she said to herself, with an appreciative accent not lost upon her only listener, "So that is *himsilf!*"

A few minutes later Truxton, having possessed himself of the two dollars, and of a voluble, if somewhat superfluous, encomium upon his late companion, took his departure. As he walked homeward, facing the first delicate flush of the western sky, he found himself making mental note of the old woman's most striking remarks. And since he was a natural mimic it is perhaps not to be wondered at that he even went so far as to repeat, *sotto voce*, that unctuous formula of farewell: "It's sorry I am to lose the swate eyes of ye, the saints save ye!"

CHAPTER V.

AN UNAMBITIOUS HERO.

WHETHER it was owing to a too immediate transition from the æsthetic delights afforded by the O'Toole art-collection, or to some still more obscure cause, the fact is worth noting that Frank Truxton was conscious of a marked change in the aspect of things when, the following morning, he entered the sober confines of the good old Pilgrim. The day was dull and lowering, and the gloom of the high-vaulted, severely furnished interior was rather accentuated than otherwise by the occasional electric light which illumined this or that dim recess.

It was close upon nine o'clock and most of the clerks were already on hand. Old Simon Barry, indeed, looked as if he had been at work all night. He always had that look, Truxton reflected, with a twinge of impatience. He wondered why a man who invariably wore a black coat, a little shiny at the seams, to be sure, but a very presentable coat as business coats go,—why the old fellow should make such a cobwebby, moth-eaten appearance. Was that the inevitable result of forty-odd years spent in the service of the Pilgrim Savings Bank? He wondered whether he should look like that forty years hence; and he registered a vow then and there that he would " get out of this " one of these days. What a deadly dull life it was, and why on earth had he submitted to it for two mortal years?

As he took his place at his desk Flynn was just placing a huge, hide-bound ledger upon it, and Truxton's thoughts were diverted for a moment, though hardly into a more cheerful channel, by the recollection that his old friend was in affliction, and that condolences were in order.

" Well, Flynn," he remarked, in a properly sympathetic tone; " I hope you got there in time to see your brother alive."

" Yes, sorr," Flynn replied, with startling briskness; " he was just haivin' his last puff! "

Even Truxton, with his lively appreciation of the old man's eccentricities, was somewhat taken aback at this blood-curdling statement. He knew better, however, than to imagine that he was thereby absolved from the expression of an exactly proper degree of sympathy, and he remarked, as he opened the ledger: " Sorry you should have met with such a loss, Flynn! "

" Ach," Flynn replied, with an expressive

shrug, " what 's the use in layminting ? No use whativer, I say ; no use whativer ! "

" That 's all very well," Truxton persisted, consumed with curiosity as to whether or not the old man was shamming. " But you 'll miss him, nevertheless."

" Miss him ? Now what for should I miss him ? "

" Well," Truxton replied, casting about for some means of self-justification, " I should think you might miss seeing him round."

" An' have n't I been seein' him round for the last siventy years—for the last siventy years, I tell ye ? " with which illogical but conclusive disclaimer, this Spartan mourner turned the subject and began commenting upon the reprehensible dilatoriness of young Beardsley, the latest addition to the gang, who was just entering the door, three minutes and a quarter late.

" You don't seem to like Mr. Beardsley," Truxton observed. " Now we think he 's a pretty good fellow."

Flynn gave the inarticulate and quite unspellable guttural by means of which he possessed the art of expressing—quite intelligibly, too—anything in the whole range of human emotions ; and then, allowing himself to descend to words, he muttered : " Pleasant, aisy-goin', good-for-nothing ! " Upon which he departed, with renewed zest, in quest of the ledger appertaining to the delinquent.

"Pleasant, — aisy-goin', — good-for-nothing," Truxton repeated to himself. "That cap fits somebody besides Beardsley!" And thereupon this usually tolerant young man, tolerant of others, tolerant of his situation in life, fairly tolerant even of himself when he gave the subject a thought, fell to abusing himself, his surroundings, and his fellow-toilers, with an animus little short of vindictive.

"What a lot of everlasting drudges we are," he said to himself, "to hang on here, doing the same thing over and over again, for a few beggarly hundreds a year! I wonder we can any of us look the world in the face!" And as if straightway to remind him what very limited significance the most aspiring philosopher is prone to give to the term he had just used, a certain pleasant and expressive countenance, not to be more precisely designated, appeared before his mental vision, quietly assuming the ambitious *rôle* which had been so arbitrarily thrust upon it.

Now it was all very well for a young man, with ideas somewhat unsettled by a too sudden initiation into the mysteries of art, to condemn himself for earning his bread in this quite unobjectionable manner, but there was really no occasion for his strictures upon other people. A pretty state of affairs it would be, if such high-flown notions were to prevail, and if all honest men were to scorn to concern themselves with the universal medium of exchange and barter, by means of which the wheels go round, the wheels of art and science and philosophy, no less than the smaller, but far more intricate ones of household and physical economy. And, indeed, what right had Frank Truxton to condemn himself for being in a situation which was the direct result of a generous and commendable course of action?

Not that Flynn's " protejay " could make any pretensions to being a hero—which, considering that he was never known to make any pretensions whatever, is not particularly to the point. His life had been too free of conflict to call for the exercise of any quality so aggressive as heroism— using the word in its conventional signification. The several crises of his modest career had been robbed of their disturbing character by the single-minded acquiescence with which they had been met.

When, at the end of his second college year, his father, Dr. Truxton, had met his death at the heels of a vicious horse, the boy's chief concern was for his mother, who, as he rightly surmised, had got her death-blow as certainly, if not as promptly, as if it, too, had been visited upon the actual physical seat of her vitality. He was an only child, and he had lost in his father a friend and comrade who had contributed even more to his happiness than his mother had ever done. Yet his own sorrow seemed to him something to be suppressed, to be roughly handled if need be, to be got out of the way at any cost, that he might have a mind free for the consideration of his mother's needs.

Mrs. Truxton was a woman of fragile constitution, and of late years the poise had become so delicate that a far less severe shock than the one she had sustained would have sufficed to turn the balance to fatal issues. Her son learned, on high authority, that the years of her life were numbered. He also learned, as a result of his own investigations, that, with the cessation of his father's professional income, the family resources were very seriously reduced. In fact, when the estate was settled, it transpired that a pitifully small number of thousands represented their entire fortune. There had been no will, and the boy found, to his indignation, that he was, in the eyes of the law, entitled to two thirds of the property. He was just turned of age, and he readily persuaded his mother to leave to him all consideration of business.

Having thus satisfactorily got matters into his own hands, he was confronted with a problem which might have proved a perplexing one to many a filially-minded son in his place. Should he pursue his education and secure his equipment for a professional life, exposing his mother, meanwhile, to the inconveniences and deprivations of an insufficient income, or, since her life was to be a short one, should he give up college, bring their capital into play, and make the scant remainder of her days as tolerable as might be? This, as has been said, might have proved a perplexing problem to many a right-minded but ambitious boy. To Frank Truxton, glad as he would have been to graduate with his class, nothing in the shape of a problem presented itself. The law was an idiot, but the money was his mother's, at least in simple human equity. As for himself, he was inclined to think that an able-bodied man would be able to earn a living when the time came, even though he were not so much luckier than nine tenths of his fellow-men as to have an education.

Meanwhile Mrs. Truxton was ordered to travel, and, for her son's sake, she entered upon a patient quest in search of that undiscovered climate which has power to heal a broken life. She found it, at the end of four years' travel, and her son had the comfort of knowing that the way had not been too hard, nor the years quite cheerless. She died in Rome, and was buried there in the lovely Protestant Cemetery.

To-day, as the young man stepped from desk to counter, from counter to desk, in the performance of the task for which he had conceived such a sudden and unreasonable distaste, his mind reverted to the hour when he had first made an important decision untrammelled by any dominant sense of duty. It was about three weeks after his mother's death, and he was on the eve of departure for home. He was going back to earn his living as best he could, for he was quite clear that he was not the kind of fellow to re-enter college at twenty-five and grind out a living in the intervals of study. It was a magnificent thing to do, but there was nothing magnificent about him, Frank Truxton.

He had gone for a farewell visit to the quiet spot where his mother slept, and, having stood for a while beside the newly sodded mound, he had wandered off under the cypresses, stooping now and then to pick the violets that perfumed the March sunshine. It was very sweet and pensive, and the tall cypresses waved their plumes with a tender, soothing, rhythmic grace. The young man strolled up the incline that rose gently to the level of the old city wall, and presently he seated himself upon a low stone coping, and fell to thinking tender thoughts of death, which seemed so gentle and friendly here, in its own quiet precincts. He remembered a letter he had received that morning, a letter written in the small, careful hand of many years ago. He reflected that the agèd woman who had written that letter was now his next of kin, and the thought warmed his heart. It had been a real consolation to him to send a cable message to Aunt Lucretia, and to feel sure that she, at least, of all the world, would share his sorrow. He drew the letter from his pocket and read it there in the shadow of the cypresses, and a fragrance of the past, of a past more remote than his memory could reach, seemed to mingle delicately with the perfume of the violets.

Truxton had only seen Great-aunt Lucretia two or three times in his life, but his visits to her, perhaps from their very rarity, had made an indelible impression upon his childish mind. He had never forgotten the old house, its decorous quiet, its generous capacity, peopled chiefly now with family portraits. He remembered a certain old apple-tree, among whose rotten branches he used to risk his neck, and the clothes-posts which he was allowed to shoot at with a deceased uncle's Indian bow and arrows. He wondered whether the holes he had made had ever been filled up and painted over; he was sure he could have placed each one. Best of all did he remember the tall old woman clad in a rustling silk dress, in the pocket of which were stored certain small, round, transparent candy-drops, calculated to make a boy forget the misleading severity of Aunt Lucretia's countenance.

Yes, it would be very pleasant to go there for a little visit, but not to make it his home, as the old lady had proposed. The hints she had dropped of an old family friend who might find him something to do were not very inspiring. But go he would, and find out whether she had kept the Indian bow and arrows as she had promised to do until he should come again.

He glanced up from the letter, and his eye fell upon the name of a well-known English writer inscribed upon a headstone near at hand. Beneath the name was a verse which he read absently, still thinking of the old great-aunt and her curious cap.

> "Lead Thou me, God, Law, Reason, Motion, Life;
>   All names for Thee alike are vain and hollow;
> Lead me, for I will follow without strife,
>   Or, if I strive, still must I blindly follow."

The young man rose to his feet with a sudden impatience, and made his way down the grassy slope and out upon the smooth-paved streets of modern Rome; and before he had got back to his lodgings he had become aware that those uncompromising lines had engraved themselves upon his memory. Was it possible that they had coerced his will as well?

> "Or, if I strive, still must I blindly follow."

Had he been such a muff, he asked himself to-day, looking back over the two years to that decision which seemed now so remote, so irrevocable,—had he been such a muff as to let his career be determined by an accident? He had come home to Aunt Lucretia and taken up his abode with her; he had accepted the place offered him in the Pilgrim Savings Bank, where he had remained contentedly enough for two years; and in taking these successive steps he was perfectly aware that there had been no decisive moment; that, literally, he had "blindly followed."

He had stayed with Aunt Lucretia because the unconscious appeal of her lonely old age made it seem natural for her next of kin to stand by her; he had gone into the great savings-bank because it was the obvious thing to do; and he had been content in both relations because he was too devoid of egotism for much personal ambition. In fact there was scarcely a situation in life, of a fairly tenable character, in which Frank Truxton, if left to his own devices, would not have fitted naturally and happily; and if, to-day, his limitations irked him, it was because he had reached that point in his experience when a subtle outside influence had touched his life and disturbed the simplicity of its tenor.

There was a gentle altercation going on between the testy Rathbone and a coy and shrinking depositor of uncertain years, who, in face of her own acknowledged signature, made some six months previous, was feebly endeavoring to maintain the proposition that she could not write.

"Now, Mrs. Brady," Rathbone demanded at last in a searching tone, calculated to wrest his secret from the arch conspirator,—"do you write, or do you not write?"

"Well, sir," Mrs. Brady confessed, with much wriggling of the shoulders and tilting of the head at a deprecatory angle,—"I suppose I do—*kind o' !*"

And Rathbone's voice dropped to a low pitch of suppressed but withering intensity as he commanded : "Then, Mrs. Brady, you will *kind o'* write your name on that line."

Truxton exchanged a glance of sympathetic intelligence with a bright young depositor who had shared his relish of the conversation, and then, much refreshed by the incident, he turned to the next candidate for attention. And it came about that under the cheering influence which the innocent foibles of one's fellow-creatures must exert upon a susceptible mind, the spirits of our modest hero made a very satisfactory rally ; with the result that, before the morning was half spent, he was wondering what he had been so disgruntled about earlier in the day.

Later, having accomplished his prosaic task with a slowly reviving appreciation of its ameliorating features, he could think of nothing more urgent to be done than to delight Miss Vickery's soul with an early return home. It was Wednesday, and he knew that it was rarely in his power to bestow a greater pleasure upon a fellow-creature than he could do by making formal acknowledgment of the old lady's reception day.

As he walked up the path between the bare stems of the lilac-bushes on either hand, he looked up, with a pleasant sense of family pride, at the fine old mansion which his grandfather of a hundred years ago had reared for the shelter of his family. The sentiment of home was a very dear and intimate one to Frank Truxton. He had long cherished an old-fashioned conviction that it was about the best thing one gets hold of in this world, and to-day the thought had taken on a personal character which gave it a new vitality, as if, somehow, it might blossom into something. He never thought of asking himself whether he had been so rash as to lose his heart, he never thought of wondering why so many stirrings of emotion had followed one another in his mind that day; but, as he placed his hand upon the brass knocker, refraining, in deference to Miss Vickery's day, from using his latch-key, the thought came to him of all the bygone hospitalities which the old brass dragon stood a symbol for, and it crossed his mind that he knew the kind of girl he would like to make a home for.

CHAPTER VI.

MISS VICKERY AT HOME.

IT so chanced that this particular Wednesday had already proved itself a record-breaker among Miss Vickery's days. As early as three o'clock, when the camel's-hair scarf was but just arranged across her shoulders, the brass dragon had lifted up his voice in unmistakable appeal, and Bridget, hastily tying a white apron over her ample form, and with but a furtive glance into the pretty old hall-mirror framed in fluted gilt columns, had opened the door to no less a personage than the brand-new minister.

The Reverend Mr. Dillaway was perhaps not in himself an inspiring personality, but he possessed the prime advantage of novelty, and his coming on Miss Vickery's day, which she had casually mentioned to him the previous Sunday, was in itself much in his favor. He was a tall, spare man of forty, of so modest a disposition that his height had always been an embarrassment to him. As he took the proffered chair, opposite his hostess, he was conscious of some misgivings as to his ability to cope with so agèd and impressive a lamb of his flock, and it was with no little trepidation that his first tentative remarks—bearing with needless emphasis upon the state of the weather—were ventured. And, indeed, Miss Vickery's appearance, encompassed by all the dignities of her day, was well calculated to disconcert a stranger who had known her only as a becloaked and bemuffled figure, stepping feebly up the middle aisle of a Sunday morning.

"Yes," she responded, affably, perceiving that her guest was ill at ease,—"yes, the weather is unseasonably warm, no doubt. I believe myself that our climate is undergoing a change"; and she lifted the feather fan in a spirit of concession to her guest's proposition.

"Yet we had a pretty cold December," the reverend gentleman rejoined, gratefully pursuing the safe and elastic theme of his choice. "There was plenty of zero weather then."

"True; but it does n't hold out. Why!" the old lady continued, with that accession of animation which marks the introduction of a personal reminiscence, "when I was a girl, in the '20's, the winter did not get his back broken until well into the spring. I remember that on my birthday, the 13th of April, 1826, we had icicles on the porch as large round as your arm;—larger," she added, with a glance in the cause of accuracy at the attenuated member in question.

Then it was that, by a half-involuntary movement, the conscious and self-depreciatory arm stretched itself forth to the red-and-gold volume of Nathaniel P. Willis's *Poems* which lay upon the table.

The Reverend Samuel Dillaway took up the book, little dreaming that he was about to score the first signal triumph of his new pastorate, and observed : " Willis was always a favorite of mine. This is the edition of 1848, is it not ? "

As Miss Vickery responded, with a delighted affirmative, the minister turned the pages of the goodly volume, lingering with due appreciation upon the illustrations, especially the picture of King David, mourning, in crown and robe, as befits a king, over the unimpeachable remains of his son Absalom.

"What an interesting character David is," Mr. Dillaway observed. " I have long had in mind to make him the subject of a sermon."

"I wish you would," Miss Vickery rejoined ; "and don't you think you might introduce a quotation from Willis? A piece of poetry seems to light up a sermon more than anything else."

" I quite agree with you, Miss Vickery, and I must endeavor to act upon the suggestion. I fear I am prone to pay more attention to the practical application of my text than to its poetic suggestion."

"You might begin with the poetry," said the old lady, the faded eyes brightening, and a hint of color touching the pure old cheeks; and then, in a voice quavering slightly with age, but finely modulated yet, and delicately incisive, she repeated the opening lines of her favorite poem.

> "The waters slept. Night's silvery veil hung low
> On Jordan's bosom and the eddies curl'd
> Their glassy rings beneath it, like the still
> Unbroken beating of the sleeper's pulse.
> The reeds bent down the stream; the willow leaves
> With a soft cheek upon the lulling tide
> Forgot the lifting winds; and the long stems
> Whose flowers the water, like a gentle nurse,
> Bears on its bosom, quietly gave way,
> And lean'd in graceful attitudes to rest."

"I don't know that it sounds much like a sermon," she admitted, "yet it seems to me a person feels better for it."

"I think anyone would feel better for hearing you repeat it!" cried the minister in a tone of admiring conviction. "I never appreciated the beauty of those opening lines before."

Is it any wonder that Miss Vickery declared it as her opinion to her next visitor—for another visitor she had on this memorable Wednesday—that the Reverend Mr. Dillaway was a man of parts, and worthy of being the successor of Dr. Miles of sainted memory?

This second caller, it should be observed, was not of that limited class for whose benefit one feels moved to repeat poetry. The lady who met the Reverend Dillaway at the front door and was thus betrayed into appearing before Miss Vickery unannounced, was the daughter of a former friend and neighbor, recently deceased.

Mrs. Hitchcock was a widow, an anxious, over-conscientious woman, quite unfitted to deal with the practical details of life. By the perversity of fate her five daughters had never had the support of the smallest slip of a brother, and, since the unseasonable demise of the late head of the house, the family had languished in unrelieved femininity. Especially in financial matters did Harriet Hitchcock feel the lack of a strong hand, and the possession of a large amount of tenement-house property formed a bond of sympathy with her neighbor of other years which doubtless had its part to play in the continuance of her friendly interest. It so happened that, to-day, Miss Vickery was led to expatiate more fully than before upon the miraculous order to which her nephew had reduced her own affairs.

"How fortunate you are," Mrs. Hitchcock exclaimed, " to have a man to look after your interests ! These agents don't seem to have any respect for a woman. You will hardly believe it, Miss Lucretia, but I have been getting so discouraged lately, that I have tried collecting my own rents."

"My dear Harriet, you never could do such a thing !" Miss Vickery protested, in open consternation. "Why, your father would *turn in his grave* if he knew it ! "

"I believe he would," Mrs. Hitchcock admitted. "Yes, I believe that he would. And Mr. Hitchcock would not approve, either. But neither would he approve of letting things run down hill. I have often heard him say that he would rather give away twenty-five dollars than be defrauded of twenty-five cents. Now if I only had a son or a nephew! I wonder," she added, dropping into a vein of painful speculation,—"I wonder why there should be so few men in the world."

It was at this juncture that the emphatic accents of the brass dragon again startled the echoes of the old house, and a moment later a welcome diversion was made by the entrance of Frank Truxton, hat in hand.

"What fine weather you are having for your day, Aunt Lucretia," he remarked, with a gratifying implication of the advantage which was sure to be taken of a sunny Wednesday; and then, by an astonishing feat of memory, he recalled the name of the visitor whom he had not seen since he was a boy.

Astonishing at least it must have seemed to a person unaware of the fact that that colorless, not strongly individualized face was indelibly engraved upon his memory by reason of its expression at a moment of extreme embarrassment which he had once witnessed. And although we cannot suppose that Mrs. Hitchcock would ever forget her sensation when her flannel petticoat dropped off, as she walked up Miss Vickery's garden-path, years ago, she must have been happily unaware of the youngster who viewed the disaster from the branches of the old apple-tree. There was therefore nothing to mar her satisfaction in the quick recognition and cordial greeting of this fine-looking young fellow who seemed at the same time so much master of himself and of the situation.

Different persons were struck by different characteristics in Frank Truxton, but few failed to discover in him one trait or another of an engaging nature. This was perhaps owing to the crucial fact which the Widow O'Toole had long since proclaimed, that he " had a way wid 'im "; and though the Puritan widow was presumably less demonstrative than her sister of Erin, she was perhaps scarcely less susceptible to the " way" which Truxton always had " wid 'im."

"Oh, yes, I remember you perfectly, Mrs. Hitchcock," he declared, in answer to her expression of gratified surprise. "You had a lot of nice little girls, ever so much smaller than I."

If an inherent truthfulness deterred him from calling the little girls pretty, his instinctive emphasis of their juniority to himself was one of those happy accidents which he was fortunately subject to. An envious friend had once accused Truxton of "unthinking tactfulness," and, indeed, there was something so transparently unpremeditated about his happiest ventures that they carried with them a conviction of sincerity.

"I am thinking of sending Louisa abroad," Mrs. Hitchcock remarked. "Some friends have invited her to join their party. Louisa has not much taste for society."

Truxton, although he recalled the rather stolid appearance of the eldest Hitchcock girl in childhood, was far too good-natured to speculate, even in his own mind, as to whether society had much taste for Louisa, and nothing could have been more candid than his tone as he replied, "I should n't think any girl's taste for society would stand in the way of a chance to go to Europe. Will it be her first trip?"

Thus launched upon a fruitful theme, Mrs. Hitchcock scarcely noted the passage of time, while Miss Vickery sat by, enjoying the occasion only the more for being relieved of all responsibility in the conversation. And by some process of unconscious cerebration, while Louisa's mother was apparently absorbed in reminiscences of her bridal trip to Europe or in the still more vivid pictures of travel which Truxton unfolded for her delectation, a resolve was forming in her mind, a resolve having immediate bearing upon the present and the actual.

"Amoroso had but one fault," Truxton was saying, in blissful reminiscence of a captivating Naples cabby, "and we succeeded in correcting that at the outset. The rascal had a way of cracking his whip which drove my mother distracted. They all do it, of course, but there was something in Amoroso's eye that convinced us that he was worth reclaiming. We remonstrated with him, and possibly our Italian was susceptible of misconstruction. At any rate he cracked the horrid thing all the louder, and we slewed round corners at a breakneck pace, until I suddenly hit upon the happy device of stabbing the villain with an umbrella in the small of the back at every crack."

"It must have hurt him dreadfully," Mrs. Hitchcock demurred; but Miss Vickery asserted with much spirit that he richly deserved it.

"We flattered ourselves that it was annoying," her nephew rejoined, gravely. "At any rate, he quieted down and became our devoted slave from that hour. I don't think he ever charged us more than double fare, and that is saying a good deal for a Naples cabby."

Was there in Mrs. Hitchcock's mind a vague association of ideas between the refractoriness of an Amoroso and that of the class of free American citizens who are prone to smash the windows of their hired residences? And did it strike her that an exercise of diplomacy of the umbrella variety might be as efficacious in a tenement-house as in a Naples cab? Possibly. By whatever process she arrived, Mrs. Hitchcock suddenly found herself possessed of the conviction that in this young man with the pleasant face and nice manners, who handled tenement-house property so easily, rested her salvation and the salvation of her five unbrothered daughters, and to her own amazement she found herself remarking, seemingly apropos of nothing, " You have a good deal of leisure time at your disposal, have you not, Mr. Frank ? "

" I 'm ashamed to say I have," Mr. Frank admitted. " I 'm always thinking I must buckle down to something out of hours. Of course," he made haste to explain, " business does not end for us clerks when the door closes, as some people seem to think. Those are the same persons," he added, " who imagine that we have all their money packed away in the safe ! "

A puzzled look came into Mrs. Hitchcock's face, almost as if she wondered where the money was kept if not in the safe. But she discreetly held to her own train of thought.

" Miss Vickery has been telling me," she said, " what excellent judgment you have displayed in the care of her property, and—I feel very delicate about suggesting it, but—could you— would you—do you think anything would induce you to collect my rents for me ? I am afraid," she added, in an apologetic tone, " that the five-per-cent. commission would hardly be an inducement to you, but—you might be glad of the occupation ! "—and the mistress of a fortune paused, quite breathless at the boldness of her initiative.

Mrs. Hitchcock had never been able to assimilate her fortune, so to speak ; it had always remained something impersonal and extraneous; the sense of responsibility far outweighed that of possession, and responsibility was something she had never been capable of handling. The late Mr. Hitchcock, keenly aware of his wife's gentle inadequacy, had been considerate enough to leave his estate in trust. It was to her father that she owed the troublesome possessions that weighed so heavily upon her spirits.

Meanwhile there was cheerful reassurance in the tone of Truxton's voice, in the very lift of his head, as he replied: "Indeed, Mrs. Hitchcock, the commission would be riches, and there is nothing I should like better—if I could do it satisfactorily. I might not have as good luck as I have had with Aunt Lucretia's property," he added, with a sudden recollection of the somewhat expensive method pursued in handling the affairs of the Broad Street block. "Hers are nearly all old tenants, and we understand each other. But I would do my best, if you would give me a few months' trial. Have you been collecting your rents yourself?"

Truxton felt as if he were inquiring of a rabbit whether he had ever tilled a farm; he had not until that moment noted the peculiarly rabbit-like cast of his interlocutor's countenance. He could scarcely believe his ears when Mrs. Hitchcock admitted that she had, quite recently, made the attempt.

"But I don't seem to have much aptitude for

the work," she added, "and I am afraid I should never learn to deal with people of that class. They are doubtless as good as we are—at least, that is what we are taught to believe—but they have different standards."

"I have noticed it myself," Truxton agreed. "And are your tenants a pretty hard lot?"

"They seem to me so; though perhaps I judge them hastily, for I have only made one attempt as yet. It was really very disheartening," she went on, drifting into a vein of mild, deprecatory autobiography. "The first woman I went to told me she had forgotten herself on the holiday, and could not pay. I was not quite clear as to what she meant, and I felt delicate about pressing it."

"She probably meant she had been getting drunk," Miss Vickery surmised, with the severity born of experience.

"I was afraid so, but I did not feel sure. Then the next woman I called upon offered me a cup of tea—it was extremely green—and was altogether so hospitable that I really hesitated to ask her for money. At the third tenement I visited, the man was so drunk that he almost knocked me over—inadvertently, I think, for he lost his balance when he opened the door. It did not really hurt me, and I did not take offence, because, of course, it is the intention that one thinks of in such a case. But I felt discouraged. I remember one woman cried and one man swore at me. I believe I only collected three dollars and a quarter, and the trip had cost me two dollars and a half for cab-fare. Since then I have been in a state of some indecision as to my best course."

Truxton had held himself sternly in check during this preposterous recital; it would never do to permit himself to perceive the humor of it.

"Have you more than one piece of property?" he asked, with admirable self-control.

"Oh, yes; and I am sure the others would be less troublesome, if I had only had the courage to keep on. This was the Launcelot Avenue block. My two mansard houses are much better and the tenants pay by the month. And then there is a row of stores on Dole Street. You remember that row of stores, Miss Lucretia? My father bought it of your family."

"I don't think I recall that particular piece of property," Miss Vickery replied, with a tinge of haughty indifference; "we have parted with a good deal of real estate from time to time."

"I am sure you are fortunate," said Mrs. Hitchcock, politely, "to have put your money into some less wearing investment. My nominal income from this property," she went on, turning to her newly acquired agent, "is something like four thousand dollars, but what with bad tenants and repairs and taxes and insurance we seem to get very little. The accounts always make a good appearance, but the checks never seem to be for a proportionate amount!"

"It 's a kind of work I like," Truxton declared; "and I have been wishing that I could try my hand at it. Aunt Lucretia's tenants are nearly all Irish, but I suppose you have all kinds."

"Yes, that is one of the great difficulties; so many of them do not speak English."

"That will give me a chance to practise the lingo. I picked up an odd lot of it while we were abroad and I rather guess I can hit it off with those Dagos and Dutchies. They talk such a jargon that they'll take me for one of themselves."

"Then you will really undertake this troublesome business?" the visitor repeated, as she took her departure, a few minutes later, filled with a mild elation at her own prowess in bringing about this astonishing solution of a difficulty.

"Indeed I will," Truxton declared, opening the door for her exit. "I shall be ready to tackle it at any time you say."

He stood a moment, watching her progress down the path; her mental excitement and the exhilaration of her spirits found expression in a quickening of her usual gait which resulted in something curiously like a series of small hops.

"Aunt Lucretia," he said, as he returned to the long parlor and took a seat near the hostess of the day, "I don't want to be disrespectful, but —did it ever strike you that Mrs. Hitchcock resembled a rabbit?"

"Oh, yes," Miss Vickery replied, with an

answering twinkle which betrayed one secret of the peculiarly good understanding existing between these next of kin. "I always wanted to call her Bunny!"

Presently, after a little desultory talk of a not too taxing nature, the old lady remarked: "It's going to be a great thing for Harriet Hitchcock to have you take an interest in her affairs; if only it will not be too much for you."

"Too much? No, indeed! Why, Aunt Lucretia, I am going to work this thing up into something big one of these days!"

There was a ring in the boy's voice of something more than good spirits, which the old lady was quick to note. She gave him a look as unusual in its sharpness and penetration as the challenge of his tone had been.

"Don't be too sanguine," she said, with grave emphasis; "that has always been our family weakness." It was the first time Truxton had ever known Miss Vickery to admit the existence of such a thing as a weakness in the family. "We always think we are going to get rich," she added, "but we never do." And somehow her nephew felt like a small boy again, and half expected her to produce a paper of smooth, slippery barley-drops for the amelioration of an enforced severity.

"Not rich in money, perhaps," he answered, gently, "only rich in work; which is better still, I 'm thinking."

Then the old face relaxed, just as it used to do after warnings in regard to apple-trees or admonitions touching Sunday suits, and Miss Vickery said, with a willing relapse into her habitual confidence: " Ah, then I have no fear; for I know that the laborer will be worthy of his hire"; and there was a tone of happy prophecy in her voice that was better than barley-drops.

CHAPTER VII.

HIGH AND LOW.

WHEN Truxton called upon Mrs. Hitchcock the following afternoon, with a view to talking things over, he found that the unassuming widow maintained a style of living which indicated wealth and worldly consequence. The house was in the fashionable quarter of the city, and if, by chance, the approaching visitor had failed to note the significant fact of its double frontage, one glance at the butler, with his air of permanence and self-possession, would have sufficed to rank the establishment. Within was an atmosphere of solid if rather heavy respectability, and, before Truxton had reached the door of the library, he had formed so distinct an impression of what the late Mr. Hitchcock must have been, that the portrait of the deceased, in black broadcloth, confronting him as he entered, seemed like an old acquaintance. So masterful was the countenance, and so lifelike too, that Truxton was in danger of overlooking the modest figure that rose to meet him.

"Yes, that is my husband," the widow remarked, as the visitor hastily transferred his attention from the past to the present head of the house. "It is considered one of Harmon's best. It was taken the year before Mr. Hitchcock died. I used to think," she continued, sighing gently, "that I should find real support in it, but—it is not at all the same thing."

As Truxton took the proffered hand, he experienced so strong an impulse of protection toward the vague and appealing little lady, that the futility of her small outburst of confidence was quite lost upon him. Indeed, it was fortunate that there could be no question of pecuniary embarrassment in this sumptuous abode; otherwise he might have felt constrained to adopt the same methods in the care of the Hitchcock property which he had employed at some cost to himself in that of the Broad Street block.

To-day Mrs. Hitchcock, though not usually distinguished for a very straight aim in conversation, had her objective point too prominently in view for indulgence in further observations unconnected with the subject in hand, and hardly were they seated before she remarked: "I sometimes have a feeling that my husband would not approve of this tenement-house property. Not that he ever expressed an opinion on the subject; but I have always been liable to very strong impressions as to what he would disapprove of. I only wish I could feel as sure of what would please him. That was always more difficult."

Truxton glanced again, involuntarily, at the strong jaw and stern eyes of the portrait. He found no difficulty in believing that the late Mr. Hitchcock had laid more emphasis upon his aversions than upon his predilections. Indeed, it was gradually dawning upon him that Mrs. Hitchcock was a widow only in name; that she was, so to speak, still subject to the marital bonds.

"Did your husband never propose getting rid of the property?" he inquired.

"He never knew of it; it came to me by inheritance after his death."

"And have you not thought of selling it?" Truxton persisted, thus unhesitatingly jeopardizing his modest business opening.

"No, I never could do that; it would seem disloyal to father. He had such faith in that form of investment, and he was almost as firm in his opinions as Mr. Hitchcock. That is my father," she added, lifting a framed photograph from the table and handing it to her guest. "He died three years ago."

The photograph was of a small, rather wizened, elderly man, with thin lips that shut like a vise. As Truxton examined it more closely he was conscious of an accession of respect for the seemingly inadequate personality of his new employer. She appeared, indeed, to lack stamina; yet she had survived the upper and the nether millstone!

"I remember your father's face very well," he said. "He used to ride a tall, bony thoroughbred. Gray, was he not, with a black spot on his nose?"

"No, my father's hair never turned; you must have confused him with someone else."

"It was the horse I was thinking of," Truxton explained. "He bit at me once when I offered him an apple, and I noticed the black spot."

"Oh, yes; old Razor had rather an ugly disposition; I was always afraid of him. So you see," with an unconsciously suggestive transition; "I should naturally not wish to cross my father, now that he is gone." And with that, Mrs. Hitchcock turned her attention to the file of accounts which Truxton was to take charge of.

Business over, ensued a tea-drinking in the family sitting-room, enlivened by four of the five Hitchcock girls, including, besides Louisa and the twins, the youngest of all, Amelia, a tall, handsome young person of eighteen, who promptly confided to the visitor that the only reason in the world why she was not out this winter like half her friends was because she had such a lot of older sisters.

"But Louisa is going abroad another year," she added, with cheerful resignation, "and we shall not have so much the appearance of a congested district."

"It is n't half so bad to be the youngest as to

be a twin," Julia declared, with a decision inherited perhaps from her father,—or might it have been from her grandfather? "When Annie and I came out we did n't have half the attention we ought to have had, because people did n't like to discriminate."

"More likely they did n't know how," the other twin remarked; "we are alike as two peas. Roland Ware told me, the night of our coming-out party, that if I would have the tip of my ear gilded, I should have all the partners."

"I should like to know why," said Julia, bridling visibly.

"Because the men would at least know which I was, while there would be nothing to distinguish you."

"I don't know why, if they knew one they should n't know the other," Louisa remarked, in exactly the same matter-of-fact tone in which she had years ago explained to Frank that "things that are equal to one thing are equal to another!"

"You don't seem to me a bit alike," he declared, with an ingratiating interest in the subject; and indeed their likeness was only that of the same landscape with and without the sun. The atmosphere was totally different.

"But they are exactly alike," Louisa insisted. "Every single feature is the same."

"Oh, the features, I grant you. But then, we all have eyes and ears and noses."

"Annie says I have n't any nose," Julia interposed, "because I don't notice fresh violets the minute I open the front door."

"I don't always notice them myself," Annie remarked, drily.

"Now, Mr. Truxton, it is your turn to be personal, just to keep us in countenance," said Amelia, with the clear, incisive utterance which she had not inherited from her mother.

"I'm ready enough to take a hand. To begin with, who is Roland Ware?"

"Roland Ware? Oh, he is Herbert Lincoln's cousin," Amelia declared, with alacrity. "You know Herbert Lincoln, the captain of the 'Varsity Eleven?"

"By reputation, yes," Frank made haste to assure her, being well aware that upon his answer depended his standing in the opinion of these rather jolly girls. He knew also that any further inquiry concerning a young man so distinguished in his cousin would be regarded as irrelevant.

"Do you go in for foot-ball?" Annie asked.

"Not particularly, though I like everything of the sort. Base-ball was my game at college," and his mind reverted, with a quite patriarchal reminiscence, to the time when he was captain of the Freshman Nine.

A far more lively reminiscence confronted him five minutes later, when, as he passed down the steps of the Hitchcock mansion, a stentorian voice struck his ear, shouting, "Hullo, Cáp.!" and he beheld his old college classmate, Will Shepleigh, making a dash across the street like an athletic ghost of the past.

"Where in thunder do you hail from?" Shepleigh inquired, in the challenging tone which had won him the nickname of "Gladiator."

"I should think it was you who were doing the hailing, Gladdy! I thought they must have got telephone connection with San Francisco when I heard your voice."

"No," Shepleigh replied, as the two young men walked up the street together; "the connection in the present instance is strictly matrimonial. I'm married!"

"You? Married? Great Cæsar! how did that happen?"

"Well, there was a general swirl of orange-blossoms and wedding-marches and gold rings, and the thing was done!"

"Of course! Only I was wondering how it came about. You never would look at a girl."

"Perhaps that was why, when my eye chanced to fall upon one, I caved," the modern Benedick suggested, with a grin which reminded Truxton of the way he used to look when he had scored a home-run.

"You always did have a flattering way with you, Gladdy. Have you ever explained the thing to Mrs. Shepleigh?"

"There was no occasion for explanations. We were both hit, and when her father made conditions we were the meekest kids you ever saw.

That's why I settled here. The old man declared he could n't live without Clara, and as I could n't either, I had a fellow-feeling, and obligingly let him take me into the firm,—Dashley, Hunt & Co., Bankers. Has a speculative sound, has n't it? But we are the safest concern in the city. My father-in-law is Hunt—fine old boy. And now, what have you got to say for yourself, Cap. ?"

"My story is strikingly similar to yours," Truxton declared, facetiously. "I also have become both domestic and practical. I reside with my great-aunt, and draw a salary at the Pilgrim Savings Bank."

Shepleigh looked thoughtful.

"I say, old man," he exclaimed, "it must have been rough on you, quitting college, and all that. We heard you had gone abroad, and that was the last of you. Why did n't you keep us posted?"

"Well, I don't know. I always did hate readin', writin', and 'rithmetic."

"You must get plenty of all three in that daisy institution you 've got stuck in."

"There are no frills to that, and I don't really mind figures."

"Ever hear from any of the old gang?"

"Nobody but Tom Sanders. Ran into him one day in New York. He 's in Colorado, doing the mining-stock trick."

"Guess they 've got a big thing out there, if

they know how to handle it," Shepleigh opined, with the judicial tone befitting a representative of Dashley, Hunt & Co.

"Looks like it," Truxton agreed; but he omitted to mention a postal-card reposing in his pocket, and bearing the mystic legend:

"Everything humming. She touched 47 this morning. Hold on for your life,"

and which, being intrepreted, meant that a paltry $500, entrusted to the discretion of Tom Sanders, had become inflated to the tune of $4700. Truxton was the last man to talk about his own affairs, and, indeed, he almost forgot he had any, in the pleasurable exhilaration of this encounter.

"Sorry that I'm off to-morrow for a ten days' trip to Chicago and St. Louis," Shepleigh remarked, as they were about to separate. "And Clara says she's going too. But — see here, Frank; we've got a dinner on for to-morrow fortnight, and Clara told me this morning we must have a new man for a feature. It's the finger of Providence, and you've got to be the feature."

"Feature! I should feel more like a freak! Do you know, come to think of it, I never went to a dinner in my life!"

"You must be hungry, then! But what do you mean? Don't you like them?"

"How can I tell? I never had a chance to try."

"Oh, I see; you don't know anybody," Shepleigh surmised, with brutal frankness; " well, it's time you did. This shall be your coming-out party. You'll make a lovely bud!"

"All right; if I can get into my swallow-tail, I'll come."

"You shall have a ticket in the morning. Bye-bye!"

"Hold on a minute," Truxton cried, after the receding form of his friend; "which arm do you give a girl when you take her in?"

"The other one," was the cheerful reply, and Shepleigh's stalwart form was already growing less in the distance.

The prospective bud was perhaps less agitated in view of his early appearance in the great world than would have been the case had the prospect opened at a less interesting moment of his business career. He had, to be sure, a grateful warmth somewhere inside of him for days to come, but it was a warmth arising rather from the genial roar of Shepleigh's greeting and the hearty grasp of his enormous hand, than from any thought of the untried pleasures which the meeting guaranteed. Meanwhile, before a second sun had set upon him in the character of Mrs. Hitchcock's authorized agent, he had become deeply absorbed in the complicated business of extracting small sums from reluctant tenants.

Truxton was not altogether surprised to find in Launcelot Avenue a thoroughfare which hardly lived up to its knightly name; yet, upon entering the rather disreputable building entrusted to his care, he found himself hailed as an old acquaintance by more than one of the denizens of that crowded human pigeon-house. And, since the depositors of the Pilgrim Savings Bank are about five thousand per cent. more numerous than its officials, it is perhaps natural that some of the ladies and gentlemen who claimed acquaintance should, in polite parlance, have had the advantage of him.

This, however, was not always the case. In old Isaac Klingstein, for example, the sole occupant of a dingy tenement under the roof, Truxton could not fail to recognize a star depositor. He was an ancient rag-and-bottle merchant who had undertaken to smuggle a second thousand dollars into the bank in the name of a fictitious daughter, and although, when confronted with his own statement of celibacy, recorded on the bank register, he had unhesitatingly declared that the daughter was an adopted niece, he was unable to bring proof of her existence, and was forced to entrust his superfluous thousand to another savings-institution of whose invulnerability he appeared to be less firmly convinced. This circumstance, which Truxton chanced to recall, taken in connection with very considerable arrears in rent, was sufficient explanation of the fact that the old man betrayed no recognition of the new agent. The chance information, however, so far facilitated Truxton's labors, that when he left the

Klingstein perch he had "cleaned up" the entire eleven dollars and a quarter due, and that he carried with him a comfortable assurance that the dollar and a quarter a week would hereafter be forthcoming.

Truxton was not without natural qualifications for the work he had undertaken. His instinctive quickness of sympathy which, if of the unintelligent variety, might have made him an easy dupe, was tempered by a certain shrewdness of perception, and he was furthermore possessed of a fund of sound common sense which enabled him to keep a pretty firm hold on the proper relation of things. If old Mother Wiley was a pathetic figure,—and that she indisputably was, with her trembling voice and her shaking hand,—Truxton was not long in discovering that she had a son who would have been well able to give her house-room, had he not indulged in the luxury of a handsome termagant to wife; and the new agent soon brought home to him the fact that if the back rents were not paid he would be forced to adopt the only remaining alternative, and stir up a domestic hornet's nest by the introduction of an alien into his household.

Yet Truxton did not scorn to humor a tenant who met his views as to probity and cleanliness. In one of the mansard houses, for instance, he found an excellent lodger on the point of departure to "a more desirable tenement." He soon discovered that neither location nor enlarged space was the attraction. From vague hints as to the liberality of the prospective landlord, he was at first led to believe that nothing short of a porcelain bath-tub or plate-glass windows formed the bait. We may fancy his joy, then, when it transpired that a magenta wall-paper which exactly matched a magnificent plush sofa, recently acquired, was the desideratum. The former agent had bluntly refused to replace a fairly good paper, and, in consequence, Mrs. Elizabeth Delay proposed diverting her fifteen dollars a month into a more remunerative channel. The lady was not easily mollified; but when Truxton, in addition to a promise of the deepest magenta to be found at ten cents a roll, let fall certain dazzling hints as to a gilt border, Mrs. Delay acknowledged herself vanquished, and the prospective landlord's schemes went up in an incarnadined smoke with lurid gilt edges.

Not that Truxton was invariably successful. Before a week was past he was obliged to own himself worsted in an encounter with a gentleman of Irish extraction, who had established himself and a cracked fiddle over a cheap eating-house in the Dole Street row. It appeared that Mr. Casey was in the habit of discoursing sweet music of an evening " down below," in return for which favor he was sumptuously fed every day; and in his scheme of life there seemed to be no more provision for rent-money than for restaurant charges. He was a genial soul, and he knew his value.

"Yes, sorr," he declared with conscious pride; "me and me fiddle, they kapes the restorang goin' most as good as if it was liquor-licensed."

He expressed entire readiness to vacate the premises, but he dropped a sinister hint as to Doherty's declared intention to quit if he did, and when a subsequent interview with the rubicund Doherty confirmed his estimate of the value to the "restorang" of the "attraction" which alone deterred him from moving his flourishing establishment to more desirable quarters, Truxton concluded that, for the present, at least, thirty dollars in the hand was worth thirty-five in the bush, and discreetly allowed the fiddle an extension of time.

And, after all, perhaps the most valuable feature of Truxton's equipment for his new work was his unfailing interest in his own kind, and his pronounced taste for studying the subject at its source. He was not much of a reader, having always preferred people to books. Indeed, he had a half-formulated theory that books were a kind of natural-history museum in which one's fellow-creatures are stuck through with pins and preserved in alcohol. Even as a boy, when he was addicted to turtles and toads and snakes, the which were sometimes found making disconcerting pilgrimages down the front stairs, he had paid but scant attention to the defunct specimens in his father's laboratory. From the first he had had a lively appreciation of the bank depositor in his purely social aspect, and his otherwise unremunerative labors among Miss Vickery's tenants had been enlivened by more than one choice example of the comedy of life. Now, again, as his field was enlarged, and as the possibilities of Launcelot Avenue and the mansard houses were gradually unfolded, he could only wonder anew at the infinite variety of human nature. Not one of the forty-odd tenants of his new employer could possibly be mistaken for one of his old friends, and so in love did he grow with their idiosyncrasies, that their appearance on the front stairs of his consciousness, so to speak, was a thing of daily occurrence.

But if the men and women, with their sharply individualized personalities, proved a mental stimulus, it was the children of the tenements that gave him the most unmixed delight. The little Micks of the Broad Street block had long since discovered that the "gintleman's" coat-pockets were a storehouse of agreeable possibilities, and we may be sure that he did not enter upon his new duties unprovided with his "baby-fodder." He was an adept at shooting a barley-drop down an open mouth, and his unerring aim in so good a cause commanded the immediate and unqualified respect of every ragamuffin in the Launcelot Avenue block. He had, too, an engaging way of insinuating one of those succulent globules between the pouting lips of the sulkiest little damsel of five, and even the "young infants "—thus fondly designated by their parents —had been known to relax their expression of preternatural solemnity, upon the insertion of a pleasing sweet between their laboring gums.

Truxton always held barley-drops in high esteem, partly for the sake of early association, but also because of their extreme lightness in the confectioner's scale. It was really amazing to find how many war-whoops of joy and inarticulate cooings of ecstasy could be purchased for fifteen cents, and if parental recognition of such courtesies sometimes facilitated the unloosing of otherwise reluctant purse-strings, why, all the better for the monthly accounts !

It must be admitted that most of Truxton's spare time during the first fortnight of his novitiate in Mrs. Hitchcock's service, was spent in the collection of the hundred-odd dollars which he gathered in; yet he felt himself amply repaid for his labors. For, apart from his satisfaction in the large number of interesting acquaintances he had made, apart from the really poignant delights it had been permitted him to dispense among the children, there was his commission to gloat over.

Truxton went over his accounts several times on the second Saturday evening, to make sure that he was fairly entitled to the nine dollars and forty-five cents which appeared to be his. Somehow it seemed to him a vastly more interesting sum than that implied in Tom Sanders's last postal-card. The card was in his pocket, and when his accounts were settled, with the scrupulous care of a bank-auditor, he pulled it out and read it again.

"Still humming. Passed 50 cts. without a sag. Can see a dollar round the corner."

"H'm!" Truxton growled, thrusting out his under lip exactly as his father used to do when he was considering the advisability of a change of medicine. He supposed he was a fool not to realize. He thought it queer that the matter did not seem more important.

"Five thousand dollars," he said to himself. "Five thousand dollars! I wonder why it looks so much smaller than that nine dollars and forty-five cents I've been grubbing over."

And at this juncture it occurred to him that he had better get his dress-suit out and have it pressed the first of the week.

"I wonder," he soliloquized, as he shook out the coat,—"I wonder whether there will be any-one there as interesting as Patsy Casey."

CHAPTER VIII.

A PLEASANT DINNER.

"A NEW man? That sounds promising," Ruth Ware exclaimed, as she seated herself beside her hostess in the Shepleigh drawing-room, to which charming apartment recent wedding-presents lent something the air of a museum of bric-à-brac. "And you are going to let him take me in?"

"Not very flattering to the rest of us," Shepleigh declared, with a self-congratulatory chuckle. Ruth was sure to be nice to Truxton.

"It's such a short time since you were new yourself, Mr. Shepleigh, that one is naturally sanguine about novelties," she retorted.

Ruth Ware was one of those girls who never look overdressed. On this occasion she carried with her an agreeable atmosphere of pale blue which perhaps had its part to play in the impression of benignity which was so reassuring to Truxton's social sponsor. She had been the first to arrive, and as she took the leisurely survey of the room which could not but be gratifying to a hostess conscious of many treasures and of some taste, she remarked, "How well you always manage your lights, Clara!"

"That is because I can't afford to sit in a glare," Mrs. Shepleigh returned, with the indolent accent derived from a Southern grandmother, and which was in marked contrast with the briskness of speech natural to the New England girls among whom she had been brought up. She even allowed herself an occasional pause in midsentence, with the result that she was not always permitted to finish what she had intended saying.

"There is only one thing more fatal to the complexion than a glare," she continued; "and that is blue candle-shades. Nobody can stand blue shades; nobody, that is, who has any objection to looking like a dyspeptic ghost. The new man," she added, as if to escape a too painful theme, "is Frank Truxton, a classmate of Will's, whom I have never met. I believe he did not graduate; his father failed or something."

"His father died, you mean," Shepleigh interposed, "and he was obliged to take his mother abroad."

"Much pleasanter, I am sure!" and the lady of the pretty drawing-room seemed to consider the subject exhausted.

"I wonder," Ruth speculated, "whether I don't know Mr. Truxton. I met a man of that name at my friend Mrs. O'Toole's a few weeks ago. Mrs. O'Toole thinks very highly of him, by the way."

"Then your Mr. Truxton is a slummer," Mrs. Shepleigh exclaimed; "I hope it's not the same one. Ah, there is a strange man taking off his coat in the hall mirror. You did not tell me he was nice-looking, Will."

"You must not expect me to tell you everything, my dear," Shepleigh retorted, with a marital sententiousness which imposed upon nobody; and a moment later Truxton entered the room in the wake of a young woman in red, with a husband of the same general complexion.

"Then you do slum!" the hostess lamented, as Ruth and Truxton gave signs of recognition. "It is a perfect epidemic among the girls, but with men one is less on one's guard."

"But, indeed, Mrs. Shepleigh, you do me a cruel injustice," Truxton protested; "I never did such a thing in my life. Who is my defamer?"

"Miss Ware. At least she tells me that you first met at her friend Mrs. O'Toole's; and you will admit that the name is suspicious."

"But, indeed, it was Miss Ware who was slumming, not I. I was merely grinding the faces of the poor. The lady, besides being one of my most valued acquaintances, is a tenant of my aunt's, and I was in the act of wresting from her a two-dollar bill. You surely can't take exception to that!"

"This is a great relief to my mind," Mrs. Shepleigh admitted, "and I only hope Miss Ware will be able to make her peace with you, for you are to take her in to dinner."

"It all seems like a fairy tale," Truxton exclaimed, as he found himself established beside Ruth in that permanency of possession which only a formal dinner can bestow. "I don't see what my fairy godmother was thinking of, not to provide me with a pair of glass slippers."

"No prince would ever submit to anything so uncomfortable," was Ruth's sagacious rejoinder; "and *apropos* of fairy godmothers, how is Flynn?"

"Flynn has a cold, I am sorry to say. He told us to-day that he was threatened with some sort of ' brown craturs in the tubes of him,' and we really feel anxious about the old fellow."

"You could hardly spare him for a fit of illness, I should think."

"Indeed, no; he is the Hamlet of the play, and we stuff him with wise saws, so that he can do justice to the part. You should have heard him yesterday afternoon, struggling with the proposition that ' procrastination is the thief of time.' "

"I don't wonder that ' the tubes of him ' got disordered," Ruth laughed.

"Oh, he got procrastination easily enough—the longer a word is the better he likes it. But he could n't seem to establish any connection in his mind between thieves and time. 'A common thafe is it, thin?' he inquired. I heard our paying-teller drilling him at it. It took half the afternoon."

"Yours must be 'a bank where the wild thyme blows,'" Ruth opined, as she added a dash of pepper to her last oyster.

"Then that herb of grace must be a four-o'clock," Truxton retorted, promptly, "for it rarely blooms before that hour!" and, as he spoke, he was visited by a reminiscence of another bit of Shakespeare, one which his father had been fond of quoting: "She was the sweet marjoram of the salad, or, rather, the herb of grace." Was it possible that that spicy, aromatic phrase had been applicable to any girl of Shakespeare's day? Truxton was inclined to think that it had been composed in a strictly prophetic vein.

"There certainly must be something Shakespearian about Flynn," Ruth declared. "And do the wise saws stay in his memory?"

"Oh, yes; they are his stock in trade. He practises each upon us until it is superseded by a new one. After he had laboriously mastered the thief-of-time proposition he sauntered up to me and remarked, in the most spontaneous manner, 'Misther Trooxton, procrastination is the thafe of time.' When I inquired where he had picked that up, he said he had known it from his infancy! I wish you could have seen the expression of his face as he turned on his heel and flung that outrageous lie over his shoulder."

"I do see it, perfectly," Ruth averred; "you were the image of him as you said it."

"If I could only believe that was true!"

"Surely you would not have a person speak the truth at the dinner-table," a voice broke in on Truxton's right. "It's against all rules."

As he turned to reply he was aware that Ruth was appropriated by her other neighbor, and he accepted, philosophically enough, such consolation as offered in the twinkling personality that claimed his attention. Miss Daisy Foxborough was of the gypsy type, with dark, woodsy hair and a clear brown complexion. There was a sparkle in the black eyes, and it was in response to that that Truxton said, "What have rules to do with a lark like this?"

"Is this a lark to you?"

"Of course it is; but perhaps you can suggest a better name for it."

"If I were to speak the truth——"

"But you must n't."

"Well, then, if I were to tell a lie——"

"That is only the reverse side of the same thing."

"Mr. Dole, help me out! You have views on truth," and the gypsy twinkled across the table in search of an ally.

"Truth," replied Harkness Dole, a man of a thin, high-bred countenance, with tense brow and a carefully trimmed beard, " truth is a relic of barbarism. It is because we are only half civilized that we do not emancipate ourselves faster."

" Why should we suppose that barbarians speak the truth ? " his right-hand neighbor inquired. She was an incisive young woman in black lace.

" It is an established fact that they do,—at least in their actions, which is the main thing. If they don't fancy a man they knock out his brains. Now, if we don't fancy a man, we invite him to dine."

" No, we don't ! " cried Shepleigh.; and then he grinned with pleasure, as he found he had accidentally said the right thing.

" Oh, you are nothing but a barbarian yourself, Shepleigh. You would make a worse botch of that particular form of civilization than the rest of us do. For of course," Dole continued, addressing his remarks once more to Miss Daisy,— " of course a lie that deceives no one is a worse barbarism than the truth ; and that is the difficulty with us who are half-civilized."

" I never spoke the truth but once," Mrs. Shepleigh remarked, in a confidential aside to Ruth's other neighbor ; " and that was when my mother asked me whether I liked Will."

" And what did you say ? " Shepleigh inquired, from the other end of the table. He was always betraying that he heard every word his wife said.

" I said I did n't know."

A ripple of laughter rose at this sedate sally,

and, as it subsided, Truxton found, to his satisfaction, that Ruth was restored to him. He made haste to say the first thing that came into his head.

"I suppose it is safe to assume," he remarked, gravely, "that these forks are arranged in the order in which they are to be used."

"I believe they are," said Ruth; "but woe to you if you begin at the wrong end, as I have been known to do. I once found myself eating duck with an oyster-fork."

"Then one survives that sort of thing? I did n't know but that a person got sent to the tower if he slipped up on the frills."

"No, indeed; nobody ever minds other people's blunders. It is only our own that worry us."

"I believe that is the truth," Truxton exclaimed, with conviction. "And at a dinner-table too!"

"I rather like to speak the truth," Ruth boldly declared. "It makes conversation a great deal more interesting—and unusual!"

"My father used to be fond of quoting an old German chap—Schopenhauer, was n't it?—who said that tongues could lie, but faces could n't. I believe he was an ill-natured old growler, but I remember one other good thing he said in that connection—that a man's words, at the best, express nothing more than a man's thoughts, but that a man's face is a thought of the Creator, and is consequently better worth studying."

"I like that," said Ruth, reflectively; "I know one or two faces that are like a thought of God"; and her companion would have been very slow-witted if he had not made mental note of the fact that he knew at least one such face.

Truxton, meanwhile, was fast coming to the conclusion that a dinner-party was the most delectable of functions. He felt as if he had strayed into a sort of fairy-land of soft hues and scents, of flowers and candle-light and delicate textures; and he found himself surprisingly at home in it. He liked the careless ease of a conversation in which it was no less natural to take part than it was permissible to keep silence. Above all, he liked to have Ruth speak to him with that friendly assumption of good understanding, and to think that perhaps he should often hear her speak, now that their acquaintance was established on a legitimate footing. What a pleasant thought of the Creator this was, this face beside him, that had first touched his imagination amid the strong contrasts of the workaday world! He thought it seemed hardly less rare, hardly less apart here among the flower of its kind.

The tide of conversation had set toward the two ends of the table, leaving Truxton free to pursue his own very agreeable thoughts. Presently Ruth, noticing his stranded condition, detached herself from the talk beyond and asked, with more friendliness than originality, "Is it a penny that you want?"

"If that is as much as you would feel justified in offering."

"Perhaps we might make it a lucky-penny."

"There it is again," Truxton heard someone say; "even Miss Ware has one!"

"Miss Ware has what?" Ruth inquired.

It was Harkness Dole who had spoken, and although his remark had been addressed to Miss Belle Duncan, the lady in black lace, it had caught Ruth's ear, as he had obviously intended that it should. Truxton had already noted the fact that this man, who never raised his voice, nor otherwise challenged attention, had the gift of commanding a hearing when it so pleased him. In fact, this was the second time that he had, without apparent effort, cut across Truxton's talk with Ruth.

"Mr. Dole maintains that we all have our superstitions," Miss Duncan explained; "and I maintain the contrary."

"What's your proof?" asked Henry Lawson, a ponderous youth, of a literal turn of mind, who had but recently become an ornament to the bar.

"My proof is, that I, for one, have no superstitions whatever."

"That, in itself, is a superstition," Dole interposed.

"Then we shall have to begin by defining our term," was the retort.

"That's another superstition," Dole insisted.

It was evidently not his first fencing match with Miss Duncan, but though she did not often succeed in turning his point, she clearly enjoyed the pastime.

"But Miss Ware has not told us yet whether she is superstitious," Shepleigh remarked, glad to take a hand in the general conversation. The lady in red had been plying him rather severely on the subject of interstate commerce laws.

"Oh, yes," Ruth declared, with great apparent ingenuousness; "I have ever so many superstitions."

"But you don't seriously believe in them," Miss Duncan protested.

"Indeed I do!"

"What are your grounds?" asked Lawson.

"They always come true."

"Please give us an instance," someone begged.

"Well, in the first place, there's the new moon. When I see it over my right shoulder I always have good luck."

"I don't see how you can remember," Miss Duncan objected, only half convinced.

"I never do," Ruth returned, demurely. "But when I have good luck, I know I must have seen it over my right shoulder, and when——"

"Oh, come! That's a sell!" cried the young lawyer, forgetting, for an instant, his newly acquired dignities; and under cover of a general murmur of amused protest Ruth made good her retreat to private life.

"You did that well," said Truxton, deeply grateful to Ruth for coming back to him.

"Thanks. And now, are you going to earn your penny?"

Ruth had the not very common gift of picking up a thread where it had been dropped.

"Oh, the penny! Well, I was taking things in. This is a new experience for me."

"Is it really so new?" she asked, incredulously, for Truxton did not impress her as a beginner.

"Yes, and no; in one aspect it is curiously like a glorified *table d'hôte*. That is the nearest I ever came to a dinner-party before."

"And how do you like it?"

"Better than I expected."

"I wonder what you expected."

"I believe I had a notion that it might seem—what shall I say—hollow. I suppose I must have read something of the kind in a book!" This in a tone which betrayed small respect for printed information.

"No, we are certainly not hollow. I know most of us really well, and we are pretty pithy."

"So it struck me. The fact is, I have been seeing a good deal lately of people who were queer or poor or vicious, and I think I had an idea that such an eminently respectable company as this might seem all of a pattern. But I find it's not the case."

"I don't know whether the discovery does more credit to your head or to your heart," Ruth jested. "But, seriously, I rather wonder at your finding anything in us on such short acquaintance."

There was no coquetry in the remark, and it may be as well to make a clean breast of it at this point and admit that Ruth was singularly devoid of that much admired quality. Humor she had and charm, and a certain lightness of touch in things of the mind, but at heart she was too straightforward to possess much aptitude for the game which is so often associated with these graces. And if Ruth's little speech was innocent of any personal tinge, her companion was equally guiltless of suspecting any.

"Perhaps Schopenhauer was my instructor," he replied, in perfect good faith. "I don't think I was going so much by what people said as, somehow, by the impression they made, apart from their conversation."

"Of course; one has to do that. The better people talk, as a rule, the less they betray themselves."

"I wish I could look about the table with your eyes," said Truxton, enviously.

"It's a pity you can't for I assure you we are very much worth while," she laughed. "But, seriously, there is hardly a single person here who is not really interesting, either in what he is, or in what has happened to him."

"Which of the two is the case with our theoretical friend?" Truxton asked, glancing across at Harkness Dole, who was taking his turn at serious conversation at the hands of the lady in red.

"Both."

"Tell me about him."

"Don't you know about him?"

"No; why should I?"

"Well, he is a good deal before the public. He is in politics, you know, and, 'by the way, a relative of mine,' as the little cat remarks in *Artful Antics*."

"That's a comfort," Truxton laughed, "for now I'm equipped with one fact, and I'm sure," he added, with exaggerated ceremony, "it's highly creditable to him! The truth is, Miss Ware," he went on, "I'm a dreadful doughhead about politics. I know your 'relative' by name, of course, and I have a general impression that he is a kind of white robin. But that is about the limit of my information."

"It's accurate, at least," she laughed; "for he really is a good deal of a white robin. That is why I am so conceited about his being my cousin."

"It almost seems," said Truxton, dismissing the particular instance, the consideration of which had somehow gone against the grain with him,—"it almost seems as if you believed that these well-dressed, well-behaved people were more worth while than the paddy-whacks and Dagos you are so devoted to."

"I do indeed," Ruth answered, with sudden earnestness; "and I believe that life is more difficult to them. I even think there is more suffering in their lives, and a great deal more effort. However," she added, recovering the tone proper to the occasion, "this is not a class in sociology; and I think you are very polite not to make fun of me."

"We *were* getting rather solemn," Truxton admitted; "but I'm afraid I began it. At any rate it interests me very much; all that sort of thing, I mean. And I'm greatly obliged to you for telling me what you have. It is so satisfactorily un-hollow!"

"If you are inclined to take it seriously," Ruth rejoined, "I ought to have confessed at the outset that I am not nearly as much given over to my paddy-whacks as you imagine. Indeed, I'm afraid they are a good deal of a side issue."

"I was beginning to suspect as much," Truxton answered, with mock seriousness. "Do you know, Miss Ware, when it first dawned upon me that you were at heart a butterfly, my last illusion fled."

"But that is an illusion, too," she laughed. "Things are a great deal too complicated for any of us to be ticketed and labelled."

"Any but the white robin," Truxton retorted, as the ladies rose to leave the table. "I consider that we have him in a glass cabinet." He did not feel at all sure that Ruth had caught his remark, but he took some satisfaction in having made it, perhaps for the very reason that it was not true; that the white robin was altogether too much alive to be a safe inmate for a glass cabinet. He was conscious of a vague resentment against the bird for being white!

"And how about that lucky-penny?" Truxton asked, an hour later, as he stood at Miss Ware's carriage door.

"Do you really think you are entitled to it?" she queried, with a severely judicial frown, which would have been somewhat more impressive without the snowy fluff of cloak and head-gear that looked so pretty in the light of a neighboring street-lamp. And then and there Truxton fairly faced the exhilarating fact that his hour had struck!

Nevertheless he rejoined, with a show of self-possession that did him credit: "That is not a matter of opinion; it is what your cousin, Mr. Dole, would call an established fact."

"Then you shall have the penny—one of these days."

"One of these days!" It sounded curiously reassuring,—as if there were to be many such days, many such evenings. He walked home under the stars. It was a cold, clear night, and the sky looked very deep and full of glorious possibilities.

"One of these days, one of these days," he kept repeating to himself. She had not invited him to come and see her; nor had she said anything which could possibly be construed into such an invitation. She had only assumed that they should meet—one of these days. There was absolutely nothing definite to look forward to, yet—how deep the sky was, how full of glorious possibilities!

CHAPTER IX.

FLYNN'S EYRIE.

THE " brown craturs in the tubes of him " would appear to have got the better of Flynn, for the sage of the Pilgrim Savings Bank had not again turned up. For two days the " spinges " had been wet by an unskilled hand whose inefficient performance of the task served but to bring into stronger relief the memory of Flynn's truly artistic methods; for two days the pudgy, impressionable old ledgers had had to submit to the less affectionate, less discriminating handling of the janitor proper,—a self-important personage who made no secret of his opinion that Flynn was little better than a cumberer of the ground; for two days no borrowed platitudes, no happy improvisations, clothed in incomparable brogue, had rejoiced the ears of the pilgrims. By the time the third day had worn to noon the matter began to assume serious proportions. It was Flynn's first prolonged absence from duty within the memory of man, for never yet had he succumbed to illness, never yet had he taken a vacation, and save for those not infrequent occasions when he had departed, wrapped in gloom, to honor the last obsequies of friend or kinsman, his figure had been as constant as that of the clock on the wall.

"Seems queer not to see Flynn round," Judson remarked, as he turned the leaves of an enormous ledger and buckled down to a column of figures. The methodical Judson was not one of those most susceptible to Flynn's charms; yet he missed him, and, what was still more noteworthy, he opened his lips to say so.

"Plague take Flynn!" Rathbone exclaimed, as he gave his sponge a vicious squeeze, sending a shower of drops over Andy Stone's carefully brushed boots. "He is n't worth much, but he does know how to handle a sponge."

"More than can be said for you, Rathbone," Andy growled.

"It is n't my business," Rathbone retorted.

"Then I 'd let it alone, my son!"—upon which, Rathbone's attention being opportunely diverted by a would-be depositor, Stone calmly withdrew the receiving-teller's handkerchief from his unconscious pocket, and, having carefully dried his aggrieved boots with it, returned it, slightly besmudged, to its natural retreat.

Yes, they all missed Flynn. Even Rand, the chief clerk, came down from the front office to inquire if anything had been heard from him, and when the treasurer himself learned of the unprecedented defection of this humblest of all the servants of the institution, he made quite particular inquiries and said: "Somebody had better look him up." Indeed, there is little doubt that if open war could have been declared upon the "brown craturs," every man of the force would have joined the expedition, breathing fire and slaughter.

The chief difficulty lay in Flynn's pronounced aversion to having his privacy invaded. The street and number of his residence were recorded on the books of the bank, but he had dexterously parried all advances looking to a domiciliary visitation, and, with all the guying of him which they permitted themselves, the men had, at bottom, too much respect for the old fellow to intrude upon him against his expressed preference.

It was known that he had lost his wife and baby soon after coming to the bank, and that he had not married again. His address had not changed in all those years, so that he had presumably continued the mode of life dating from his marriage; but whether he had anyone to look after him and give him his meals, or whether he foraged for himself, was a question shrouded in mystery.

Truxton, who had decided to adopt Saturday evening for the collection of Mrs. Hitchcock's rents, was so haunted by thoughts of his old friend, as he groped his way up and down the dimly lighted stairways of the Launcelot Avenue block, that he determined to brave the displeasure of the jealous householder and find out just how things were going with him. He had that morning looked up the address, which proved to be ominously near the unsavory thoroughfare with which Mrs. Hitchcock's business interests had familiarized him.

Wondering very much why an acknowledged capitalist like Flynn should not allow himself more desirable quarters, Truxton made his way to the dingy old barracks where the pilgrim sage housed. It was a large and many-windowed edifice of decent brick, with five main entrances, flush with the sidewalk. As Truxton opened the door of No. 41 he encountered a damp chill that was far more penetrating than the frosty air outside. He knocked at the first door on the right which, after some delay, was opened by a girl of ten, with pinched features and precocious eyes.

"Can you tell me where Barney Flynn lives?" he asked, lifting his hat to the small woman who, in some occult manner, impressed him as a personage.

"Third floor above this. Guess he's away; ain't seen him since two, three days."

"Thank you."

"Say, mister, be you a missionary?" the child inquired, as Truxton turned to go.

"No, I'm not; why do you ask?"

"I thought p'r'aps you 'd come in and pray with pa. He 's drunk, and when he 's drunk he cries easy an' sometimes he signs the pledge."

This startling request was accompanied by such an earnest, supplicating look, that Truxton, muttering, "Sorry I can't fill the bill," beat a hasty retreat lest he should be constrained by those remarkable eyes to assume the alarming *rôle* imputed to him. His progress was not without its perils, for the stairs and balustrades were shockingly out of repair, and an unwary step might have disastrous results.

Arrived at the top of the house, he groped his way along the passageway to the door which had been indicated to him. There was no answer to his knock, but, as he turned the handle, the door opened, to his infinite relief, and he found himself in a fairly large, square room, across which the rays from an electric street-light cast a spectral radiance. The room was bitterly cold.

Truxton drew a match from his pocket and lighted a lamp which he discovered on a high bureau between the windows. Almost at once he heard a feeble voice call, "Katie, Katie; are ye there, darlin'?"

With a stricture of the heart Truxton picked up the lamp and, shading the light with his hand, stepped into the adjoining room. There, in a huge four-poster, piled high with obliterating comforters, the face of the delinquent sage was just visible, looking curiously small and shrunken, in spite of the outcrop of beard which was beginning to bristle about the chin.

"An' is it yoursilf, darlin'?" the feeble old voice inquired.

Truxton placed the lamp on the floor at the foot of the bed before speaking. Then he stepped to the bedside and took the old man's hand in his, saying, "It's I,—Truxton. Don't you know me, Flynn?"

The patient did not return the pressure of the hand, but he began blinking and muttering, gradually feeling his way back to consciousness. The sound of Truxton's voice seemed to call into his face a ghost of the old kindly and tolerant humor that was curious to see, and gradually his mutterings, though still inarticulate, took on something of the rising and falling inflection peculiar to his speech. Somewhat reassured, Truxton turned his attention to practical matters.

There was no direct means of heating the little bedroom, but in the neat kitchen beyond he found a large cooking-stove, and a good supply of fuel. Also the larder was well filled, showing, among other delicacies, a boiled ham, still intact, stuck full of cloves, the ornate arrangement of which testified to the artistic leanings of Flynn's chosen caterer. A jug full of milk, flaked over with frost in this cold storage, was presumably sweet, and there was plenty of tea and sugar. All these things and more besides were carefully arranged upon the shelves of a narrow cupboard, and, even in his haste and anxiety, Truxton was struck by the order and the scrupulous neatness of the little establishment. It was difficult to believe that all this comfort and decorum existed beneath the roof of a neglected tenement-house, and it was still more incredible as the creation of a single unaided man.

When the fire was well ablaze, and the kettle on, Truxton, not without a self-congratulatory surprise at his own prowess, returned to the bedside. The blinking and muttering had subsided, and Flynn greeted him with a grunt of full intelligence.

"Well now, Misther Trooxton," he remarked in a tone of assumed indifference, "have yez nothing betther to do wid yoursilf than that?"

"Not a thing, Flynn," Truxton answered, wishing that he dared lay profane hands upon the old man's person, for the purpose of straightening out the bed-clothes and knocking up the pillows. But there is a limit beyond which only the foolhardy will venture, and Truxton, on this occasion, elected to cultivate that better part of valor which is tacitly recommended in the old proverb. This, however, did not prevent his assuming a valiant air of nonchalance as he said: "In about ten minutes you're to have a cup of tea and give an account of yourself."

"An' if ye takes my advice, Misther Trooxton, ye'll go home!"

"But I have n't the least idea of taking your

advice," Truxton replied, as jauntily as might be. Then, drawing up a cane-bottom chair, and establishing himself upon it, he opened fire in good earnest.

"Flynn," he demanded, "where's your doctor?"

"How do I know that?"

"Have you seen him lately?"

"Seen him?"

"Yes; have you seen him to-day?"

"An' how should I be afther seein' him, an' me layin' here stuck fast in me bed like a pig in a bog?"

"Who is your doctor, Flynn?"

But Flynn had exhausted either his strength or his patience, and, closing his eyes, he lay still as a graven image.

Now Truxton had inherited something of that native sconce which no training can give, the possession of which had formed an invaluable feature of his father's professional equipment, and, after watching the non-committal old face intently for a few minutes, he came to the conclusion that there was nothing very serious the matter here. The patient was not coughing, and his voice, though hoarse, was not much worse than it had been when he first made mention of the "brown craturs." In short, the self-constituted attendant was inclined to believe that by one of those miracles that are daily performed in behalf of the poor and the ignorant, the bronchitis had been averted, and that the old man was simply enfeebled by cold and hunger. The adoption of his own diagnosis greatly simplified the treatment of the case—a fact which any skilled practitioner will find it easy to credit !

Accordingly, when the tea-kettle had begun to hum, Truxton, still greatly pleased with himself, prepared a cup of tea and proceeded to administer it with a quasi-professional zeal that was not to be withstood. He got his patient propped up in bed and wrapped about with a big comforter, and the tea was straightway imbibed, though with many a protesting grunt. The result was so far a success that, by the time a second cup of that innocent beverage had disappeared whither good tea goes, the old man was sufficiently revived to put in a demand, on his own account, for more solid food.

With some slight misgivings Truxton suggested ham, and the avidity with which several slices of that succulent viand were consumed carried with it something so reassuring that a hint as to a "coople av apples" that would bear baking was blindly followed.

Pending the preparation of these last, Flynn settled back among the pillows, and presently an unearthly trumpeting, broken into curious staccatos and falsettos, proclaimed that the old man was at peace with the world and, by inference, with his own internal organism.

Truxton, still further reassured, picked up the

lamp and strolled into the front room. It was still very cold in there, but the room had a cheerful aspect. In the two windows were well-worn curtains of turkey-red—a fabric which preserves its brave aspect, even in its declining years—while the upholstery of chairs and sofas was done in bright Brussels carpeting.

On the wall above the sofa hung a life-size photograph of a girlish head. It was apparently enlarged from a tintype or some such trifling form of portraiture, and there were those curious lapses in the impression which frequently occur where a portrait—or a personality—has been forced too far beyond its natural limitations. Yet, none the less, the character of the face was preserved, and Truxton knew well that the pretty, sentimental eyes, the long, sentimental curls, no less than the short upper lip and the piquant nose, were the very features of "Katie."

Under the picture was a small wooden bracket screwed against the wall, and, in a blue glass vase upon it, a few fading flowers hung their heads. It would have been a dull mind that had missed the little romance of the old tenement, and, as Truxton turned from the contemplation of the picture, he stepped more softly than the patient's physical condition would have seemed to demand.

And if, a half-hour later, when the baked apples had followed the tea and the ham upon their consoling pilgrimage,—for Flynn had promptly waked in response to the pungent odor of the crisping skins—if Truxton then went forth to the nearest drug-store and sent a telephone message to Miss Vickery announcing his absence for the night, the step was prompted less by anxiety as to Flynn's physical welfare than by the wish to keep a very lonely old man company.

It is doubtful whether Flynn himself realized very much of what was going on that evening. After the first excitement of seeing Truxton, when he had roused to something of his habitual attitude of mingled self-defence and toleration of others, he had become comparatively quiescent, and, by the time his hearty repast was quite finished, he had settled down into a wholesome lethargy which augured well for a night's repose.

Truxton, more content than ever with the situation, set himself to washing up the dishes, a function which was not without pleasant associations with camp-life. Indeed, it was in that out-of-door school that he had acquired the semi-domestic handiness which stood him in such good stead on this widely dissimilar occasion. His task accomplished—with no less satisfaction for the picturesque contrasts it offered — his thoughts turned to a well-earned repose, and he cast about for some available substitute for a bed. Attracted by the structural conformity of the carpet-covered sofa to the requirements of the human frame, he confidingly established himself upon it ; but he was not long in coming to the conclusion that the springs of that deceptive piece of furniture were created less for the purpose of yielding to pressure than of resisting it, and after five minutes' trial they became so incisive in their remonstrance against an unaccustomed burden that he sprang to his feet and sought a more pliable resting-place.

The warmth of the kitchen stove was agreeably suggestive, and he at last found complete satisfaction in three wooden chairs. There was a smoothness to their hard surface which compared favorably with the eccentricities of the sofa, and when at last he was comfortably ensconced upon one of them, close to the stove, his legs spread over the remaining ones, he felt himself in the lap of luxury. He did not venture to light a pipe, lest its odor should prove as rousing to the patient as that of the baking apples, and before he had begun to think of sleep he was dreaming incoherent dreams.

After what seemed about ten seconds of time Truxton was waked by Flynn's voice in the adjoining room. The lamp had burnt itself out, but there was brilliant moonlight in the bedroom. The old man seemed to be talking in his sleep. Truxton leaned over him and asked if he wanted anything. He could see in the moonlight that the old eyes opened, but they closed again and the lips moved. Truxton leaned closer and listened.

At first only a few stray words were intelligible

—the name of Skibbereen, of Katie, of Pat, and again of Katie. Once the sweetest smile came about the old lips in the dim light, and Truxton, waiting for Katie's name, heard them say, "Granny, darlin'!" The mind had strayed far afield in the shadowy regions of the past.

Truxton drew a chair close to the bedside and sat for a while thinking that the old man might be near to waking, and presently there was a movement as if he had really roused, and he began to speak quite distinctly. But it was in a tone of happy reminiscence that he said, "A little place, a coople o' miles out, where the pipers used to coom an' pipe."

After that ensued a pause, yet the regular rise and fall of the breath in slumber did not recommence, and again Truxton heard him speak, in a still more natural tone of voice.

"They called it—what 's that they called it, thin?—the *randyvoo!*" Upon which, with the satisfaction which the conquest of a long word never failed to infuse into him, the old man turned on his side, and presently the regular, heavy breathing, gradually becoming vocal, indicated that the patient slept.

For a long time Truxton held watch beside the bed, while tender thoughts visited him of Katie, with her long curls and sentimental eyes, thoughts and imaginings that were not to be frightened away by any unmelodious sounds. To the accompaniment of portentous snores the light young figure of long ago seemed moving about the quiet rooms. He could see her righting this and that, he could fancy her decking herself for high-mass. Half-dreaming, yet with the moonlit room still visible, he seemed to see the pretty figure glide past him into the little kitchen and bend over the stove, and, so strong was the impression, that Truxton, recalled to himself, involuntarily sprang to his feet and took a look at the fire. It was getting pretty low, and he replenished it, picking up the pieces of coal between his fingers and putting them softly, one by one, into the stove. Then he went back and resumed his seat by the bedside, and fell to thinking, not of Katie, but of another young and comely face in a setting of candle-light and flowers and soft textures. Yes, he thought to himself, the best things in life come to rich and poor alike—if they but come ; if they but come !

Flynn moved and spoke.

" A sup o' wather, darlin' ! "

He drank the water with eyes still closed, and this time he returned the affectionate pressure of Truxton's hand. He did not question whose it was—perhaps he knew, perhaps not. But one thing was surely plain even to the sleep-confused intelligence : it was a friendly hand that he had hold of ; for the first time in many a long year " the ould man " was not alone.

CHAPTER X.

A PHENOMENAL CURE.

IT is doubtful whether the medical profession, with all its science and industry, has yet discovered in ham and baked apples a sovereign cure for bronchitis. The brotherhood is notoriously shy of domestic remedies, and perhaps with reason. In the case of Flynn, however, this primitive treatment proved a complete success, and, by the time morning broke, those two familiar and comforting agencies, assisted by a snug sleep, had infused through his enfeebled system a new warmth and reviving vigor.

When Truxton awoke on his hard couch, with stiff legs and a momentarily bewildered mind, the first thing he took note of was a strong odor of tobacco. Glancing through the open door into the next room he discovered his patient sitting up among the pillows, in the grim dawn, tranquilly smoking a clay pipe. Truxton sprang to his feet in consternation and strode to the bedside.

" Great Scott, Flynn ! where did you get that

pipe?" he demanded, with the severity of a trained nurse who had been overreached by his patient.

"I slapes wid it under me piller," the culprit replied, with entire suavity and composure. "It's warmin' to the insides, of a cold marnin'!"

There was not a word of comment upon Truxton's unaccustomed presence, not a word of gratitude for his care. Flynn merely regarded him with his old, kindly indulgence, while he answered, laconically but tolerantly, such inquiries touching his health as the self-appointed attendant instituted. Even when Truxton turned his attention to domestic details, and proceeded to replenish the fire and to fill the tea-kettle, the master of the establishment offered no remonstrance. He only settled a little further back among the pillows, and pulled at his pipe in a contemplative manner.

Presently the rattle of milk-cans was heard below, and Truxton, with commendable presence of mind, hastened in pursuit of the passing vendor. He came back, flushed with triumph, and bringing with him, in addition to the milk, a gust of keen, frosty air.

Flynn greeted his entrance with an approving nod and remarked, his pipe still between his teeth, "Your honor's as spry on your feet as hersilf!"

Over and above this unprecedented use, on Flynn's part, of the courtesy title, the force of the allusion itself was quite overpowering, and

Truxton was dumb. He hastily repaired to the kitchen where he deposited the milk on the window-sill, and then, returning, and taking his pipe from his pocket, he established himself at the bedside for a social smoke. The spontaneous association in the old man's mind of himself and Ruth had been curiously gratifying, and Truxton was conscious of a sneaking hope that it might be followed up by something further in the same vein. But Flynn was too much of an artist to run a good thing into the ground.

They sat for some time in a thickening cloud of tobacco-smoke, while the tea-kettle began to hum, and a democratic sparrow on the window-sill chirped as lustily as if he had been privileged to disturb the slumbers of the rich. Little by little the neighborhood awoke. A man's and a woman's voice rose in altercation through the floor; a boy whistled beneath the window. Once in a great while a cart rumbled by, but there was little traffic in the streets of a Sunday morning.

After a while, seeing that the old man had smoked his pipe out, and become more available for social purposes, Truxton judged that the time had come for a tentative remark regarding the immediate future of his patient.

"Flynn," he asked, abruptly, "what do you say to letting me send round a nice woman I know to look after you for a few days?"

"Me? An' a nice woman? An' lookin' afther me?"

No printed words, indeed no human speech save Flynn's own, could do justice to the supreme contempt with which the echo of those three propositions issued from the depths of his being.

"You would n't like it?"

"Naw, sir, I would *not!*"

"But Flynn, you 're a sick man. You 've got to be looked after."

"A sick man is it? And what for should I be a sick man?"

"Why, you 've got bronchitis, have n't you?"

"Sure an' it 's not a tinimint-house that I am!" he exclaimed in explosive remonstrance; and then, thoughtfully refilling his pipe, and pursuing with much satisfaction the suggestive metaphor he had stumbled upon, he added; "Anny ways, I 'm thinkin' they 've took notice to quit, the unhatherly bastes!" After which highly imaginative flight on the part of the pilgrim sage, the two friends smoked in silence, while Truxton regarded his patient with a critical eye.

It was broad daylight now, and he was struck by the change in the old face. There was a serenity of expression in it that was almost beautiful. The countenance, to be sure, was still a perfect cat's-cradle of wrinkles, and the color of youth would never return to the furrowed cheeks. Yet it seemed as if certain lines must have been softened, or as if there had been a change in that subtle modelling which only a skilled artist can reproduce, and which can scarcely be defined in words. To reduce it to plain terms, Flynn looked rested. It crossed Truxton's mind for the first time that perhaps the old man had felt the stress and strain of life; perhaps even the handling of ledgers and fetching of luncheons, and the parrying of home-thrusts might pall, after forty-odd years of unintermittent service. The "brown craturs in the tubes of him" had clearly wrought no permanent harm; was it not possible that the enforced idleness had wrought positive good?

"You do feel better, don't you, Flynn, honestly?" Truxton asked, in a tone calculated to entrap confidence.

"Betther is it? Sure it's the spinges I'll be wettin' to-morrer!" and for a fleeting instant the fire of youth seemed to light the old eye.

"We missed you like everything, you know," Truxton continued; "everybody was asking after you—even Mr. Seymour made inquiries."

But this was a climax of improbabilities which proved too great a strain upon the old man's very limited credulity, and he relapsed into a less enthusiastic mood. "That 'll do, that 'll do," was the sceptical response.

"Fact!" Truxton asseverated.

Yes, Flynn was better; indeed, he was "out of it," as Truxton told himself, with no little satisfaction; and if the sponges were destined to submit yet a few days longer to the manipulations of an unskilled hand, the patient, meanwhile, throve and prospered as a convalescent.

A Phenomenal Cure

He would have no dealings with doctors or nurses or hospitals, and Truxton had not the heart to press the matter. In fact, although the latter was an assiduous visitor and nurse during the entire period, and although the sense of intimacy with the old man grew, yet he could never rid himself of the feeling that he was really an intruder, and that it behoved him to move circumspectly. Also there was a look as of the wisdom of ages in Flynn's eyes, such as one sometimes sees in the eyes of a very new baby, which made his " protejay " feel excessively young and inexperienced.

For a day or two Truxton looked in, morning and evening, with an eye to feeding and warming and airing the patient; but by Monday afternoon he found the old man up and dressed, and his bed made up with clean linen.

Now Truxton had gone to a greenhouse on Sunday, and got some pinks and mignonette with which he had surreptitiously replaced the faded flowers in the blue glass vase. He wondered whether Flynn would comment upon them, and, if he knew better than to look for any conventional word of thanks, the fact only lent a zest to his expectations. In the meantime, they conversed on many topics of everyday interest, including the disreputable condition into which the tenement-house had sunk.

" An' it 's a shame it is," Flynn declared, waxing eloquent ; " a foine pace of property as anny in the city, wid thirty-six windies to the front of it, wan for ivery day in the month!"

But of the flowers no word was spoken until just as Truxton was taking his departure.

"You are sure that there is nothing I can do for you, Flynn?" he asked; "nothing I can get for you to make you more comfortable? You are sure?"

"I am that," was Flynn's emphatic rejoinder; and then, pulling a match out of his pocket to relight his pipe, he added, "An' your honor 'll not be afther wastin' your money on anny more bowkays for the likes o' me. It 's mesilf that thought yez had more sinse!"

Yet if Truxton's harvest of thanks was but a scant one, the fact was of small moment to him. The unaccustomed situation had, of itself, been most fruitful of interest and amusement. As he looked back upon his own emotions at first finding the old man in his momentarily pathetic condition, and on the promptness with which the suggestion of tragedy had got itself turned into comedy, he found himself becoming sceptical as to Fate ever getting a serious grip upon Flynn. The debonair manner in which he had encountered the "brown craturs" seemed to augur well for his nonchalance under a more serious crisis.

To be sure, there was Katie, and the old tenement, the portrait, the flowers in the blue vase! Yes, Fate had certainly found him out once, unless all signs failed; and Truxton had imagination enough to do full justice to the evidences of the fact. That a man so fastidiously neat as Flynn should submit to the malodorous, uncleanly character of the house; that so old a man should risk his life on those rickety stairs; above all, that one so self-respecting, and of so much innate delicacy of feeling should continue under the same roof with drunkards and slatterns—all this implied some potent influence, not superficially apparent. And although the long curls and the pathetic eyes of the young creature, dead close upon forty years, might not in themselves have afforded a testimony conclusive in a court of justice, the fading flowers in the blue glass vase left no room for doubt.

Truxton's already awakened interest in tenement-houses found much sustenance in this particular example. If the house did not boast quite the palatial character which Flynn was inclined to claim for it, it was at least a fairly good piece of property, which had been outrageously neglected—criminally neglected, Truxton told himself, with the extravagance of youth, which, by the way, is quite as likely to be right as the hesitancy of age.

Even after his visits to Flynn had ceased—and he knew better than to continue them beyond a certain limit—he carried about with him the thought of that wretched human hive, and this served at least the good purpose of spurring him on to fresh endeavors in behalf of both landlord and tenant of such property as he had control of. In so much that there speedily came a time when that artistic relish in the foibles and the humors of his kind, which had originally played so large a part in his satisfaction, was in great measure superseded by an interest which came perilously near being philanthropic.

Meanwhile, as his acquaintance with Ruth Ware progressed,—and it was of far too spontaneous and unconventional a nature to halt at so favorable a moment for development as that afforded by the Shepleigh dinner—he found in her no lack of stimulating interest. His formal admission as visitor in the Ware household had come about very easily and naturally.

One day, about a week after that memorable night-watch, in the course of which the thought of Ruth and Katie had become so curiously associated in his mind, Miss Ware came in to make a deposit on three or four books. Thanks to the complicated machinery of the bank, the duty of returning the books to her devolved, not upon the receiving-teller, but upon Truxton, who joyfully seized this opportunity for a word with her. As he handed her the little bunch of books he remarked, in a strictly business tone: "I don't know whether you are aware that one of the fundamentals of sound finance is a prompt payment of debts. You incurred an obligation at our last meeting."

"Oh, the penny," she replied, with such unimpeachable gravity that the watchful Flynn, intently observing the interview from a remote corner, was forced to the prosaic conclusion that it was business "hersilf" was talking. "It is customary, in the financial circles where I have got my experience, for the creditor to come and collect. I am sure my mother would be glad to know any friend of Margaret O'Toole's";—a concession to the unique origin of their acquaintance which broke through the seriousness of the conversation in a manner profoundly gratifying to Flynn.

A few minutes later, when Truxton had returned to his desk, the old man, unable to refrain from some exhibition of sympathetic intelligence, sidled up to him, and remarked, in his deepest guttural, "I seen her wid me own eyes, comin' out of the Tripe tinimint wan day, an' me a-standin' on the stairs an' not stirrin' hand nor futt." Then, finding his information tolerated, —and indeed Truxton was far too elated at the moment to resent anything—he waxed eloquent and declared, "An' the Tripe gyurl, she throwed her arms around the waist of her an' burst out a-cryin'!"

"The Tripe girl?" Truxton repeated. "Is that the thin little wretch with the big eyes and the father that drinks?"

"It is that sorr! An' hersilf she just stoops down an' takes the gyurl's face in her two hands an' kisses her; an' she says, says she, 'There,

there, Mattie, I'll come again to-morrow, sure I will!' Faith, an' it's no place for the loikes of her—a dirty low tinimint an' a drunken idjit an' no woman about the place at all, at all!"

"Not a very good place for the little girl either, I should think; eh, Flynn?"

This heresy was too much for the equanimity of the pilgrim sage. With a grunt and a grimace he abruptly turned on his heel, and sought refuge in the cellar, there to commune with the bank cat in whom he had long since recognized a kindred spirit.

It must be admitted that Truxton himself rather wondered at the turn his own sympathies had taken. Far from deprecating the appeal of the poor little wretch, clinging so pitifully to the skirts of her one friend, far from sharing Flynn's sense of the unfitness of the situation, he found all his sympathies enlisted for the child. Ruth was strong and wise, and to his mind she could no more be injured by intercourse with the poor and the unclean than an angel from heaven could soil his wings in an earthward flight.

Yet Truxton did not for a moment compare Ruth to an angel. He felt that she was altogether too delightfully human to suggest high-flown notions of other spheres. He liked to think that her strong, shapely hands were not too white, not too delicate for helpful deeds; it was good to know that the face about which he had woven so many dreams and fancies, the face which was to him a "thought of God," need not shrink from contact with the poor, thin, worn little face of the drunkard's child. He was willing that she should shine like the sun, alike upon the evil and the good—and then he remembered, with a thrill of exultation, that she had expressed her willingness to shine upon him, who was neither evil nor good, neither rich nor poor, but only a commonplace bank-clerk, with no legitimate claim upon the dispenser of such rare gifts.

Truxton had bought a little bunch of pinks that morning of a boy in the street. They stood in a glass on his desk. He liked flowers, and the boy had looked as if he would like ten cents. From time to time as he got off from the counter and returned to his work on the trial balance—knitting-work, Aleck Plummer used to call it—he would take a sniff at the flowers. They were uncommonly spicy, and he wished he had been at liberty to hand them to Ruth. Perhaps she would have stuck them in her dress—that dark-green serge would have made a capital background.

Presently, when bank-hours were over and Flynn, having long since emerged from his chill retreat, sauntered past, bound for home, Truxton exclaimed, "Here, Flynn, have a posey!"

And as the old man graciously accepted the offering, even conceding that it was "a very dacent bit av a bowkay," his "protejay's" mind recurred, with much satisfaction, to the image of the blue glass vase, and to the face of Katie above it.

CHAPTER XI.

THEORY AND PRACTICE.

IF Ruth Ware was, in one phase of her character, something of a philanthropist, she was almost as unconventional a one as Truxton himself—and this fact the two young people discovered, to their mutual satisfaction, very early in their acquaintance.

"The beauty of your theories," he said to her one evening, "is that there is nothing painfully rigid about them."

"No, I am afraid there is not," she replied, regretfully.

"Afraid there is not?"

"Yes; if there is anything I delight in it is a theory; but I could never make one work."

It was a lovely evening in the latter part of April, and the long windows were open to the floor. They gave upon a balcony overlooking the quiet square, and Truxton had an unchastened desire to get out there with Ruth, who, for her part, was sitting contentedly enough just within the muslin draperies, with the light from a street-lamp striking across her face. It ought to have been moonlight, but the effect, to Truxton's eyes, was really just as satisfactory. There were tall, spreading elm-trees in the square, and their delicately budding lower branches caught the humble light from the street-lamp as gratefully as if they had been all unaware of the stars shining among the upper boughs.

A game of whist was going on in the adjoining room, and Truxton glanced from time to time through the wide folding-doorway, with real commiseration, upon Ruth's elder sister, with her three companions, handling those unpoetic pieces of pasteboard, oblivious alike of the stars in the branches, the fragrance in the air, even of the light on the face of Ruth—poor things! He did not pause to consider that those four persons were, for the moment, presumably content with their situation, while he—he wanted to get out on the balcony!

Truxton had come to feel very much at home in this pleasant old house on the quiet square. Its inmates, though perhaps not individually very remarkable people, formed, collectively, a delightful household. Mrs. Ware herself was a serene and kindly matron in whom one seemed to discover the source of the more genial of the qualities appertaining to her widely diversified brood. For if neither Sarah, the whist-player, who was frankly bookish, nor Elsie, delightedly dancing her first season through, had the advantage of resembling Ruth, yet each and all seemed imbued with their mother's genius for easy hospitality.

The two elder sons being absent, in the cause, respectively, of matrimony and foreign travel, there remained, of the boys, only a serious-minded freshman, a youth who promptly attached himself to Truxton with that stubborn, inarticulate devotion which is the prerogative of animals of the nobler kind. Caleb never talked about Truxton, and rarely addressed a word to him, yet his feeling was as unmistakable as if he had declared it. The boy's name, in its solid staidness, was more appropriate to him than to his father, Mr. Ware, senior, being sharper-witted, and of a quicker, more peremptory temper than this youngest of his children.

Truxton's status in this as in other families whom Shepleigh introduced him to, had been not a little promoted by the discovery of ties of family acquaintanceship of a generation or two back. His name was an unusual one, and such genealogically minded of the elders of society as recalled the fact that a daughter of old Squire Vickery's second son had married a Truxton, were quick to verify the inference that this pleasant young fellow possessed the advantage of a grandfather. That this was an advantage, cannot be denied, and, indeed, it would have been too much to expect that the world at large should share Ruth's idiosyncrasy, and base its regard for a stranger upon his connection with the O'Tooles and the Flynns of the social order.

As for the young man himself, he was not, as we have seen, indifferent to family traditions, and he was especially gratified to know that Ruth's grandfather had been a classmate of one of the Vickerys, and had visited at the old house in his college days. Yet Truxton did not lose sight of the fact that it was to Ophelia Pye and the widow that he primarily owed certain quite inestimable privileges.

Meanwhile, as he watched Ruth's face in the light of the street-lamp that pleasant April evening, he found himself in some danger of forgetting his manners. It is always easy to be silent when one's eyes are well employed.

Ruth, for her part, did not appear to consider the conversation urgent. Having made her little statement of fact she seemed in no haste to expatiate further.

"Tell me one of your theories," her companion asked, at last.

"One of my theories," she said, thoughtfully, as if her mind had, nevertheless, been pursuing the subject in the interim,—"One of my theories is, that the Tripe family ought to be broken up. You remember Mattie Tripe? According to every known and accepted theory, those children ought to be put into a home. But I can't bring myself to have it done."

"Why not?"

"Because Mattie is engaged in saving the souls of the four boys. That sounds absurd, but it is not. Nothing else in the world could keep those boys straight. Last summer, for instance," she continued, leaning forward a little, in the growing eagerness of narration, "we had hardly got Mattie and the two younger ones off for a country week, when Dan and Jimmy proceeded to get drunk and to fight one another like tigers, and they kept up that sort of thing pretty much all the time she was away. They had never done it before, and they will never do it again—as long as Mattie stays with them. I can't make out whether they idolize her or whether they are afraid of her."

"Perhaps it's her eyes," Truxton suggested. "You remember I told you how she looked at me when I inquired for Flynn's tenement. I never was so alarmed in my life!"

"I remember that you ran away!" Ruth laughed. "Happily, the boys have more nerve! She will probably die," with a sudden seriousness, "but I think not at present. She would not allow herself to until she felt safe about those boys."

"Isn't it rather a pity that she should have to?" Truxton asked, and he watched Ruth's face for the answer.

"A pity that she should have to die? Oh, no; she has earned the right, poor little soul! It would be heavenly to see her asleep."

A man need not have shared Truxton's partiality for Ruth, to feel the indescribably tender compassionateness with which this was said. It was not the lightly flowering pity that may be grown in a shallow soil. It was deep and genuine and vital, and Truxton felt himself so stirred in spirit, that, in very self-defence, he took issue with her.

"It seems a little cruel, though," he said.

"From our standpoint, yes. But the child has a right to follow her star."

"Do you think she knows that she has a star?"

"Oh, no; all she knows is, that the boys need her. And she is right; Mattie is always right, and—she does follow her star, all the same. Do you see Jupiter up there?" she asked, with a seeming change of subject. "It looks as if he were caught in the elm-branches—but he is not."

"I wish we could get her and her star out of that house," said Truxton, recognizing the continuity of Ruth's train of thought. "Flynn says it is really a very rough crew there."

"I am afraid it is. But perhaps it will not always be so, for I was told yesterday that that block of houses was in the market. It is always possible that it may fall into better hands."

"That is the best news I have heard for many a day!" Truxton exclaimed. "Do they hold it pretty stiff?"

"I fancy not, for they are selling it to settle an estate."

"I wish I could get hold of it."

"Indeed I wish you could. I asked my father if he could not buy it and get you to manage it."

"And what did he say?"

"He said he could, but he would n't!"

"And I would, but I could n't! That's Fate, all over!"

"Yes, Fate is very unbiddable"; and at that, Ruth left her seat and stepped out upon the balcony. Truxton followed her with the most delicious sense of having got what he wanted.

"There is one consolation," he remarked, as he leaned against the balustrade and followed the lights of a passing cab, conscious of a lively compassion for its inmates, whoever they might be; "Fate sometimes gives us what we want without our asking!"

"True," Ruth replied, with a deep sigh of satisfaction; "I am sure a person would have to be a poet or an artist, or some such inspired being, to ask for anything as lovely as this evening."

Then Truxton, having got a chair for Ruth, seated himself upon the stone balustrade, privately blessing the thermometer for recording an unseasonable warmth. The talk trailed off, in a desultory manner by way of the temperature, the visitor repeating Miss Vickery's historic statement regarding the icicles which had adorned one of her early birthdays. He was always glad to quote Aunt Lucretia; it seemed in a measure to restore her to her rightful place in society.

"I wish we knew your aunt," Ruth said; "and I don't see why we don't. Julia Hitchcock says they have always known her."

"That is because her grandfather was a neighbor of my aunt's. Propinquity counts for so much."

"Yes; and I suppose it has got to be so while we live in such a crowd."

As if the words had evoked the crowd which had, up to that moment, been kept at bay, a tall figure came striding along the sidewalk, and just checked itself, Truxton thought, in the act of turning to pass up the steps of the house. Harkness Dole had seen them on the balcony, for he lifted his hat and passed on. Truxton knew that he was a frequent visitor at the house, but it had not before occurred to him to resent the fact. Yet the impression had been growing upon him for some time past that a cousin was a nondescript kind of creature, with a tremendous pull over other men, especially when he had succeeded in creating illusions about himself.

"I wonder why Harkness did not come in," Ruth speculated, in a disengaged tone.

"Perhaps he is tired of seeing me round. This is the third time he has met me here."

"I suppose you have met him here just as often," Ruth retorted, carelessly; "so I don't see but that you are quits. And, by the way, he is not exactly a cousin. He was only my aunt's step-son."

"Oh, is that all?" Truxton returned, in a transparently chagrined tone. Then, recovering himself, "Aunt Lucretia says she does not believe in second marriages, because they are so confusing!"

"Tell me more about Miss Vickery. I should think an old lady named Lucretia must be very much of a person. Is she as dignified as her name?"

"Yes, she is obliged to be very dignified, in order to keep things going. It always seems to me that she took a certain attitude when the circumstances of her life made it the natural one, and as if she had shown quite remarkable backbone in not modifying it in the slightest degree, now that circumstances have changed. She told me one day that she could not remember that anyone had ever been impertinent to her in the whole course of her life."

"I should like to know her," Ruth said.

"I hope you may—one of these days," and Truxton's mind reverted with a warm sense of satisfaction to the time when Ruth had used that phrase with reference to the lucky-penny.

Not that anything so sordid as a copper coin had ever passed between them; yet it seemed to him that its promise had been quite wonderfully fulfilled. Perhaps Louisa Hitchcock was right, —perhaps things that were equal to one thing were equal to another!

And before the week was out Truxton had verified one, at least, of the agreeable correspondences suggested in Louisa's classic speech, for he had established the existence of a highly satisfactory equation between a certain real-estate investment and a hitherto uncertain mining speculation.

To be more explicit, he lost no time in making inquiries about the projected sale of that "foine pace of property wid thirty-six windies to the front of it." He discovered that it could be had for the taxed valuation, and on easy terms, and upon investigation it proved to be in better condition that was superficially apparent. The main foundation and walls of the structure were solid, the general system of plumbing was sound, and Flynn's eyrie was warrant of what might be done with the individual tenement.

Negotiations were pending for a month, tests and estimates were making, and, about the middle of May, Truxton braved the mingled contempt and chagrin of his Colorado correspondent and sent orders to realize on the bulk of his miningstock. His old classmate, imagining that he had become nervous over some recent fluctuations, expended large sums in the telegraphic transmission of facts as to smelter returns, and fancies as to coming dividends. But Truxton was firm, not to say peremptory, with the result that within a few days a draft on New York for nearly nine thousand dollars went to swell his usually modest bank-balance, giving a short-lived air of importance to his pass-book, before playing its part in bestowing upon him the dignities and responsibilities of real-estate ownership.

Truxton, with his customary reticence in such matters, confided to no one the outcome of his mining venture; indeed no one had been really certain that such a venture had been made. Nor did he think it necessary to give out the fact that he was now trying his luck in real-estate. For his own part, he found this new form of investment much more to his taste than the questionable methods and phenomenal ups and downs of speculation, in which he had always had an uncomfortable feeling that somebody was sure to get hurt,—that his gain must be somebody's loss. Here, again, what was equal to one thing usually turned out to be equal to another! He found his respect for Louisa Hitchcock growing, perceptibly, so that the next time he called upon the family it was with a half-defined hope,—destined to disappointment, — that this hitherto unappreciated philosopher might add some other valuable axiom to his slender store.

To do Truxton justice, his deepest satisfaction in his new acquisition arose from the thought of the power he had acquired of giving some twenty families of his fellow-creatures a comfortable home. He knew it was a task that he could handle, and that sentiment of home which was innate in him could not but be gratified by this impersonal indulgence of it.

He proposed to continue, indefinitely, the mortgage, which was proportionately small enough to go at a low rate of interest, and, for the first year, he purposed spending money freely in repairs. His salary was amply sufficient for his present needs, and if, one of these days ?—there had been one miracle,—who could tell ? Perhaps Louisa's philosophy hid a yet unsounded depth ! Perhaps a fortune that had shown itself equal to one miracle might prove equal to another !

The day on which the deed was signed and Truxton came into formal possession, he remarked casually to Flynn, " That block of houses where you live has been sold, and the purchaser has put me in charge. We must try and straighten things out there; eh, Flynn ? "

The old man gave his " protejay " a coldly critical look.

" An' it's yoursilf the new landlord has putt in charge ? "

" That's the idea, Flynn ; what do you say to the arrangement ? "

" Well, sorr, ye 're full young, but," with a shrug of the shoulders, " I belave ye manes well ! "

" Flynn, you 're no good ! " Truxton cried, really dashed by this cold-blooded sententiousness. He had been so ill-advised as to indulge in pleasurable anticipations of that moment, and for once he was deceived by the old man's feigned indifference.

How much he had been deceived he learned, a

few hours later, when Rathbone confided to him Flynn's cautious summing up of his character. Without any word of introduction or elucidation, the pilgrim sage had remarked to the receiving-teller: "That young Misther Trooxton now! He's a plaisin', modest gintleman, but he's *shrewd*, now I tell ye, he's *shrewd!*"

The extravagance of this compliment, considering its source, was wholly unprecedented, and Truxton could not but admit, with all due modesty, that he must henceforth be considered to outrank the gang!

CHAPTER XII.

TRUXTON'S UTOPIA.

TRUXTON'S choice of Flynn as his first confidant was due no less to his being the only one of his associates available for the part, than to the fact of his close personal interest as tenant. The new householder did not care to impart intelligence of so agitating a nature to his aunt. Not that she would have been in the least degree disturbed by the character of the investment itself; indeed, it was quite what she had been brought up to, and that alone would have been warrant of her approval. It was the mortgage that formed the stumbling-block. Frank might have been as cautious as he would, the existence of this feature of the transaction would surely have got itself revealed to her, and a mortgage, in the eyes of Miss Vickery, was nothing short of a blot on the 'scutcheon which no self-respecting family would for a moment tolerate.

As for Ruth, Truxton naturally did not speak

to her of the negotiations while pending, and by the time his purchase was completed she had passed hopelessly beyond his reach, swept away by that tide of emigration to shore and hill and country-side, that annually depopulates certain sections of our cities. The Ware family were wont to go into retreat, as it were, for five or six months of the year, in an old country house, quite out of calling distance, and Truxton knew very well that, for all practical purposes, or for such purposes as from his standpoint were practical, they might as well have taken up their residence at the North Pole.

For some days after his farewell call in the old elm-grown square, he reflected gloomily upon the irksomeness of a civilization which deterred him from flinging all conventionalities to the winds, and besieging the family in their isolated stronghold. Gradually, however, his mind became so preoccupied with plans and processes for the regeneration of his property that, had not the thought of Ruth been inextricably associated with the very details of his work, her image might have receded somewhat into the region of dreams. Even so, he soon found that his last thought at night and his first thought in the morning,—and it must be owned that, at this stage of his experience, there existed for him no intervening hours,—his first and last thought, then, was not, when should he meet Ruth again, but, what should he have accomplished for her approval ? No ; Truxton, as might have been foretold, was no disconsolate lover in the absence of his mistress. The part would not have suited him, even if he had had the leisure to play it.

As the long summer with its great heats and merciful respites held its course, he found himself pressing the business of landlord with all urgency, and with an exhilarating consciousness of success. It was all very modest, this work that he was doing ; to the indifferent spectator it might have seemed sordidly prosaic. Yet to Frank Truxton it was anything but that. That sense of power had entered into him which makes a man feel himself a genuine factor, however small a one, in the general scheme of things ; that consciousness of usefulness which makes the homeliest task worth while. And how could any work be prosaic that had got itself inextricably associated with the thought of Ruth ?

One afternoon in August Truxton was walking along his street, as he unconsciously called the dingy thoroughfare in his first pride of possession, when, as he approached his own block of houses, a most amazing thing happened—a thing which might fairly be called a miracle. The door of No. 41 opened, and there emerged therefrom, not an angel from heaven, not a fairy godmother, not even a queen in crown and sceptre— but something far better. For it' was no other than Ruth herself, clad in rustling garments of lilac cambric, and wearing a hat adorned with lilac-blossoms. As she recognized him she hastened forward with unmistakable cordiality.

"O Mr. Truxton, I am so glad to see you!" she cried. "Can you tell me who it is that has bought this house and is doing such wonderful things to it?"

"Modesty forbids," was his solemn rejoinder, as, with anything but a solemn countenance, he possessed himself of her hand.

"You have bought it yourself! I might have known it!" and, as if she could now refuse him no good thing, she considerately ignored the fact that he had not let her hand go.

Not to press his advantage too far, Truxton loosed his hold, but only to establish one of a less tangible nature.

"Are you in a hurry?" he asked. "Could you come in and look things over and give me some hints?"

"Yes, indeed; there is nothing I should like better, and I have plenty of time on my hands. Mamma and I are spending the night with the Dunbars, at Fairfields, on our way home from the Cape."

"And you have been to see Mattie Tripe?"

"Yes; all she could tell me was that the new landlord looked something like a missionary, but that he never prayed with Pa!"

This was repeated with a little gasp of amusement, ending in a laugh on either side, the joyousness of which was hardly accounted for by the grotesque suggestion of the precocious Mattie.

They had entered the furthermost of the five doorways, and Ruth took things in at a glance.

"You 've painted and varnished the walls," she exclaimed. "What a happy thought! How clean and light it is! Oh, but you 've put glass into the house-door. What a difference it makes!"

"Does n't it?" Truxton agreed, with ill-disguised triumph. "It makes a different thing of the entry. I let a tenement on this floor last week, on the strength of those two panes of glass, to such a jolly German family. They were tickled to pieces over it. Now come up-stairs and see my star-chambers."

"You had to put in a lot of new steps, did n't you?" Ruth observed, as they passed up the stairs.

"Yes; you can see where they are new. But the others are clean, though they don't look so;" and Truxton paused, anxious for a response. If Ruth should feel doubtful about it there must be an entire new flight at once.

"Don't I know?" she answered, with a little wise, experienced inflection which commanded Truxton's entire confidence. "Why, the feel to your feet is different."

At the top of the first flight of stairs they knocked at a door which was opened by a tall, bony Swedish woman, of whom Truxton demanded the keys to No. 3.

"That is the only altogether respectable tenant besides Flynn that I found in the whole block," he said, as the woman disappeared for a moment. "She keeps the keys and shows the rooms to applicants who come out of hours. You lock things up pretty promptly, Mrs. Mattesen," he observed, as she handed him the keys. "The paperers can't have been gone more than fifteen minutes."

"Yes, I locks him early, or de rooms do be full of womans to see de new papers!"

Nothing could have been more withering than the accent of disdain with which the word "womans" was enunciated.

"I wish I could think of any way of knocking a little light into this stairway," Truxton remarked, as he passed on in advance of Ruth. The stairs had never seemed to him so dark. "But I've got a scheme on for ventilation that promises well. This is the only empty tenement I've got to-day," he continued, throwing open the door of a little room behung with pink paper; "though I suppose I've got to turn out one family in No. 41."

"Not the Tripes, I hope?"

"No; they don't make trouble. Besides, Tripe has braced up like everything since you gave him that music-box. It's a curious thing, but that fellow makes a perfect fetish of it; he will sit and listen to it by the hour. Did Mattie put you up to it?"

"Yes," Ruth answered, as she stepped from chamber to chamber of the clean little place, poking an inquisitive but approving nose into closet and sink and stovepipe hole. "Yes, Mattie told me that the only thing that her father liked better than drink was music. So I sent that over, and told him that if he would get twenty dollars into the Pilgrim Savings Bank for Mattie before the first of October I would make him a present of the music-box."

"I had no idea you were so clever at bribery and corruption!"

"You have yet much to learn," she laughed. "The beauty of it is, that the book is made in my name as trustee, so, while he can put in all he likes, he can't draw a dollar. Mattie says he has n't been so steady at work for many years. Poor little mouse! As if she knew anything about 'many years'!"

"She sometimes looks a thousand years old," Truxton demurred.

"Yes, and sometimes about two. How nice this all is, Mr. Truxton!"

"Do you really think so? And why won't you sit down on something? Here!" and, taking off his coat, Truxton flung it over a board that the paperers had left across a couple of barrels. He was glad he had on an outing-shirt and no waistcoat, and he remembered that he had rather admired his necktie that morning when he put it on. Truxton was no dude, but, like many an older and presumably wiser than he, he made something of a cult of his neckties.

"Thank you, Sir Walter," Ruth exclaimed, taking the proffered seat; "and now tell me all about it from beginning to end."

"In the first place, how do you like the paper?" asked Sir Walter, throwing open a window and seating himself on the ledge, whence he had an admirable view of the apparition in lilac which was making itself so much at home in the rose-colored box of a room.

"It's pretty," she replied, with an emphatic nod; "and the next room is different. They like that, just as we do. I never could see why such people must have their bedrooms and parlors and kitchens all papered exactly alike. You'll let this fast enough."

"Yes; Mrs. Mattesen says so. She is so delighted with things that she gives the house a great character. She gave me to understand, yesterday, that there was only one 'out' in the whole establishment."

"And that was?"

"*Cockrats!*" This in a sepulchral whisper which was so good a piece of mimicry that the uncanny image of a cockroach rose as promptly in Ruth's mind as it had in that of the horrified young landlord. "Miss Ware," Truxton inquired, with great seriousness, "can you suggest a remedy for cockrats?"

Whereupon Miss Ware unfolded all the lore

which she had gathered in several years' frequenting of the chosen haunts of that direful denizen of the water-pipes, and Truxton listened as devoutly as if the theme had been of roses and humming-birds — more devoutly, perhaps, for what have roses and humming-birds to do with the one vital question which alone, at that moment, seemed worthy of consideration?

The sun was still shining across the open space at the rear of the house, and a long ray came slanting over Truxton's shoulder and just touched the toe of Ruth's neat shoe and the hem of the lilac gown. He hoped that his guest noticed it, for he thought its appearance highly creditable to the establishment.

Presently, the grewsome subject of the "cockrats" being satisfactorily disposed of, conversation took a more pleasing turn, the master of the property unfolding an ambitious plan for a roof-garden which he hoped to put into execution another summer. He narrated, with much spirit, how the idea had been suggested to him by a family of Galician Jews, who had asked permission to keep the Feast of the Tabernacles on the roof —only the men, not the women—and how they had erected an arbor of lattice covered with cloth and wound with living green, and had slept and supped there for three days and nights—only the men, not the women.

"If you have a taste for revenge, Miss Ware," he added, with mock seriousness, "we might admit only the women, not the men, to the roof-garden."

Miss Ware promised to give the subject her best consideration, but, meanwhile, might she not see the roof? And Truxton consented, with a doubtful glance at the lilac cambric.

A few minutes later, when the transit had been accomplished with impunity to limbs and lilacs, he and Ruth found themselves standing on a breezy height, commanding a view of chimney-pots and attic-windows, with a splendid arch of sky overhead, and a glimpse of the river at the end of a narrow opening. They were both familiar with some of the famous views of the world, but to Truxton, at least, no Alpine heights had ever given quite the thrill of joy that emanated to-day from those chimney-pots; and Capri itself, sleeping upon the bosom of the Mediterranean, had scarcely seemed as fair as the old coaling-schooner, in the narrow glimpse of river, that gently swayed its masts to the pulse of the incoming tide.

Ruth was full of inquiry and suggestion, in the light of which they could almost see the roof-garden grow before their eyes, and at last she said, with an unconscious implication which was almost too agreeable to be overlooked: "I do think, Mr. Truxton, we shall be able to make something really fine up here—always provided that you are not going to ruin yourself. I wish you would tell me something of the business aspect of the thing—that is, if you don't mind."

"Well," Truxton admitted, as he watched an eight-oar scull cross the narrow strip of river; "the business aspect is rather a limited one for the first year. I shall get out the fixed charges and these repairs, and that's about all."

"I don't suppose my father would approve."

"Perhaps not. The fact is, Miss Ware, I owe it to the estate. You may say it's a debt I did not contract; but I assumed it, which comes to the same thing."

"Of course you did, and it was in order to assume it that you bought the property!"

The conversation was going on as easily as if the natural place for the discussion of grave questions of finance and philanthropy were among the chimney-pots of a tenement-house.

"In one way it has been good business," Truxton remarked, with a jerk of his head toward a tall adjoining building to the northward, whose solid brick rose two stories above them. "The owner of that block over there has asked me to take charge of it. He lost two tenants to me a week ago, and he came in to see what we were about."

"Shall you do it?"

"Not as manager for him. I have offered to take a five-years' lease and handle it independently. I can do better work in that way, and it will be more profitable."

"You will have your hands full," Ruth remarked, a few minutes later, when they had safely accomplished the descent of the first perilous flight, and were passing down the dark stairs to the street-door.

"That's what I like," he declared, adding, as they stepped outside, "I mean to go in for real-estate altogether, one of these days. It's opening up so fast that I can almost see my way clear to it already."

"You mean that you would give up the bank? I should think you would feel as if you were throwing away a season-ticket to the theatre."

"But it would never do to spend your life at the theatre,—and then,"—with a comical grimace,—"there is something dreadfully inelastic about a salary! But I don't know why I should make you listen to my visions, unless,"—and he looked into her eyes with a sudden impulse, as suddenly suppressed, to tell her then and there the true meaning and inspiration of all his work,—"unless I could conjure up something more poetic than anything I have been able to muster yet!"

"Poetic!" she repeated, as she took his hand in parting—for here their ways diverged, and Truxton was too ardently desirous of walking to her father's office with her to venture to do it. "Poetic!" she repeated; "there's more poetry in the work you are doing than in anything I know!"

"If there is any poetry in it," he cried, with a

backward toss of the head that seemed to Ruth very expressive, "it is of your making, Miss Ware."

"Then you will tell me more some time?"

"Yes; one of these days!"—and as she passed down the grim city street, in all the country freshness of her cambric gown, Truxton strode away without once turning to look after her.

And, indeed, where was the need? Did he not see her clearly before his eyes, for hours after? And all that evening, and for days to come, his happiest fancies moved as in a lilac haze, and there sang in his ears, in many tunes and many keys, his own confident prophecy,—"One of these days, one of these days!"

CHAPTER XIII.

AN UNLUCKY WINDFALL.

"BLESS my stars and gaiter-boots!" cried Andy Stone, with an elocutionary vigor worthy of a more forceful expletive; "if the old Pilgrim ain't just painting the town red!"

It was close upon the stroke of nine, and Andy was gazing with awestruck admiration at a stencilled design, of decorative intention, which was springing into being under the eaves of the Pilgrim's high-vaulted interior. It must be admitted that Andy drew somewhat upon his imagination, as, indeed, he was prone to do; for the design to which he paid this tribute, far from being of a martial hue, was done in a subdued mouse-color, against a background of the faintest possible hint of pearl.

"There's life in the old bank yet," Wilkinson opined, with the comfortable chuckle which only the very stout know the secret of.

"Since we set up a boy, there's no telling what lengths the board may go to," said Harvey

Winch. "Here, Tim, take these letters out to the box."

"Yes, sir!"

The boy, a meagre-looking youngster of fifteen winters—he had not the appearance of having enjoyed any summers—sprang forward with an alacrity which presented a favorable contrast to the somewhat cumbersome movements of the janitor proper, to say nothing of Flynn's air of studied leisure. Up to this time, but one fault had been discovered in Tim,—he chewed gum every hour of the day. Moved by Truxton's dismal suggestion that it was probably all the nourishment he got, the men had allowed him to chew on, unmolested, though to the stricter disciplinarians of the gang—Rathbone, for instance, and Polly Voo—such an indulgence accorded ill with the dignity of the institution. As to the higher bank officials, Tim was too small to come within their range of vision at all.

"They do say," Truxton observed, as he opened the cash-box, and busied himself with a parcel of bills,—" they do say that we are to have new light-shades next month."

"That's what I call an orge of extravagance," Andy Stone declared, turning, in response to the first applicant of the day, who thrust out her book, between the leaves of which a lonely dollar bill was secreted.

"You wish to make a deposit, madam?"

"Naw, sir; I wants to putt it in!"

This carefully explicit lady was speedily followed by others, of greater or less familiarity with business terms, and conversation ceased. It was the first Saturday in September, and things were pretty lively for all concerned, owing to the vacation absence of two of the clerks. Truxton had petitioned for the latest possible date for his fortnight, being anxious to get his own private affairs in running order before quitting the field. He was about to start by the Monday boat on a trip to Nova Scotia with Stone and Rathbone, and meanwhile he had been acting as Plummer's substitute. It was his first experience as paying-teller, and though he found it strenuous work, he liked it. And although, under the pressure of unaccustomed responsibility, he could not abandon himself as freely as usual to the enjoyment of his fellow-creatures and their vagaries, yet he found his task not devoid of human interest.

Truxton possessed a readiness of resource which stood him in good stead in his dealings with the recalcitrant depositor. It was aptly illustrated on this very morning, when there appeared before him a well-dressed and moderately intelligent woman, bearing an order for a hundred dollars, to be paid on the book of an absent depositor. Unfortunately for her, there was some irregularity in the signature which made it impossible to honor the draft.

"I am very sorry," Truxton declared, with the patient sympathy which he was never too hurried to bestow upon a disappointed applicant; "but you will have to send this back and get it properly signed."

"Well," she exclaimed, after some futile protest,—"well, I don't suppose anybody can make the Pilgrim Savings Bank do anything it does n't choose to,"—and there was arraignment in the very pronunciation of the bank's name and title, —"but, if you 'll excuse my saying so, it seems to me there is about as much difference as there is between tweedledum and tweedledee."

"You 've hit it exactly," Truxton exclaimed, in his most candid manner; "the whole effort of the bank, in these little formalities, is to make sure that Tweedledum does n't draw out the money of Tweedledee. And you have no idea," he added, confidentially, "what a sharp lookout we have to keep for the sake of both parties!"

The depositor's face cleared. Either the picturesqueness of the proposition, or Truxton's beguiling good temper had won the day, and the good old Pilgrim was restored to favor with a friend of many years' standing.

"You did that very neatly," said a grave, approving voice, close at hand, and, looking up, Truxton caught a friendly twinkle in no less august an eye than that of the treasurer-in-chief. This important personage was an unusual apparition at the counter, and Truxton gave him a nod of pleasant good-comradeship which the old gentleman relished mightily.

Mr. Rufus Seymour thought he remembered that this was the man who got his place on the recommendation of the late Sam Reynolds. Bright fellow the young chap seemed to be. Must have a level head, too, or Smith would not have trusted him with the paying-teller's work.

"Could you spare $10,000 in bills?" the treasurer asked. "They 've run short at the Seventh National next door, and have sent in to us."

Truxton probably owed this explanation, which took place while he was counting out the required amount, to the fact that Sam Reynolds and Rufus Seymour used to snowball each other in the early '30's. He took a gold certificate for $10,000 in return for the bills, and, placing it in the drawer, reverted to the humbler details of his work. He was too inexperienced to know that the transaction was an unprecedented one, or that the cash-box had probably never before entertained so portentous a lodger.

The weather was oppressively warm, and presently Truxton got hold of Tim and sent him to fetch a linen coat which he kept on hand for such exigencies of temperature. Seizing a leisure ten seconds he stepped behind a friendly pillar, and accomplished the transit from one coat to the other, and those ten seconds proved to be the limit of his recess for that morning.

To Flynn this busy day was a very tedious one; for, while the throng at the counter was not sufficient to confer upon him the brief authority of sheep-dog, his various friends were too fully occupied to pay him the attention which he pretended to scorn, but which was, in reality, meat and drink to him. To-day he was not even sent forth after that midday provender, the gathering of which was one of his most highly esteemed functions, and, when it became clear that it would not be permitted him to forage for his " protejay," he sank into a mood of deep dejection. This, however, could not long endure in a sage of his fertility of resource, and at last, taking matters into his own hands, the old man sallied forth, and presently returned triumphant, concealing something under his coat-tails.

Edging close up to Truxton he whispered, with his most insinuating inflection, " Sure, sorr, ye 'll step up back there and take a taste of tomato soup ! "

" Great Scott, Flynn ! what should I want of tomato soup ? " Truxton exclaimed ; and then, as the pungent odor assailed his nostrils, and it dawned upon him that the old fellow had actually invested his own capital in this unfortunate selection, he added, good-naturedly : " That is, I have n't got time, just yet. Set it away somewhere, till I can turn round."

Only half approving, Flynn proceeded on his way, all unconscious that his pail was leaking, and that drops of scarlet fluid marked his progress over the floor.

"Here, Flynn, what have you got there?" asked James Judson, as the dripping apparition passed his desk.

"Nothing, sorr, nothing at all," Flynn replied, with haughty reserve; and it is on record that not a smile flickered across Judson's serious countenance, as he watched the progress of the culprit, noting, with cold disapproval, every gory drop that decorated his path.

But Rathbone summoned Flynn, and told him that if he did not wash up those bloody tracks he would be indicted for murder; upon which the pilgrim sage, with a sceptical "I doubt it!" wandered off in search of Tim.

Now, in Tim's mind, the old janitor's authority was as unquestioned as that of Mr. Seymour himself; more so, in fact, for the treasurer seldom had occasion to exercise authority over Tim, whereas Flynn appeared to labor under the impression that the new boy had been expressly engaged as body-servant to himself. Accordingly the youngster was promptly set to work obliterating the signs of guilt, laboring, the while, quite as industriously with his gum-blest jaws as with his scrubbing hands.

"An' yez had better kape an eye on Misther Trooxton, and clane up under his desk whin yez gets the chance;" with which admonition Flynn, quite exhausted, returned to the consideration of the *Morning Trumpeter.*

At last it was two o'clock and the great doors

were closed. One by one the remaining depositors found their way out, Flynn opening the door with careful calculation as to the exact space requisite for the egress of each figure. The bank officials, too, took their departure, Stone and Rathbone among the first to go.

"All aboard at twelve on Monday," Andy Stone called, in cheerful accents, on his way past Truxton's corner.

"Boat ahoy!" came the response from Truxton, as he tied up a parcel of bills, and made a jotting of amounts on a slip of paper.

It would have seemed that the boat might shortly be called into requisition on *terra firma*, for a portentous thunder-storm was gathering. Truxton was so absorbed in his work that he hardly noticed how dark it was growing; yet he mechanically turned up an electric light over his desk and went on with his count. Each time the door was opened and closed a gust of wind came in; but the refreshment of it was more noticeable than anything else in the close interior, redolent as always of the masses, with, to-day, a strong admixture of turpentine.

There had been an unusual amount of business transacted for the season of the year, and it was after three o'clock before the cash was straightened out. At last the orderly packages of bills were stored away in the cash-box, the gold certificate being fastened by a separate rubber-band to the top package, that it might at once attract

Plummer's eye, when the lid of the box was lifted.

Meanwhile, a great hammering at the front door made itself heard above the rolling thunder, which was now in full voice, and just as Truxton was about to close and lock the box, preparatory to carrying it to the safe, a telegram was handed him. Its contents must have been of an agitating nature, for his mind became, for the moment, entirely detached from his cash-box, and as the door opened for the departing messenger, and a great gust of wind swept the counter, he was still too absorbed in his telegram to notice the snapping of a certain rubber-band, and the simultaneous rising of one of the bills, as if on wings. They proved to be but futile pinions, and the paper, borne down, perhaps, by the essential earthiness of filthy lucre, fluttered feebly to the floor at Truxton's feet. He, all unconscious of this ambitious but abortive flight, returned in a moment to the business in hand, closed and locked his box, deposited it in the safe, and then departed, with a preoccupied nod of farewell to Simon Barry, the last of the force remaining at his desk.

A moment later, Tim, who was in no haste to go out in the rain, bethought himself of Flynn's command, and, getting an old sponge, repaired to the paying-teller's counter, his mind bent upon that which is next to godliness. Next, perhaps, but, alas! too far removed, on this occasion;

for, as he stooped to his work, his eye fell upon a crisp bank-note, curled up in the shadow, and, seized by an altogether ungodly impulse, he picked up the bill and stuffed it into his trousers pocket.

The act was a purely precautionary one. The boy could not decide at once upon any particular line of action, but at least he would keep the game in his own hands. He gave but a glance at the bill as he pocketed it, but that glance was sufficient to reveal the fact that it was nothing less than a "tenner," a sum which represented untold riches to his dazzled imagination. Yet his short service at the bank had been sufficient to impress him with the immensity of its financial resources, and it seemed to him quite possible that the loss even of a "tenner" might pass unnoticed.

Still down upon his knees, and scrubbing with deceptive zeal at the already spotless boards, he glanced furtively about the place. The painters had stopped work at noon, and the only living creature besides himself in that great interior was Simon Barry, standing at his desk with his back to Tim. It was hardly probable that old Barry had eyes in the back of his head, though such weird fancies are pretty sure to suggest themselves to the mind of the evil-doer. But then, as Tim might have reasoned, in his dim substitute for an intellect, he was not yet an evil-doer. Of course he had to pick up the bill and put it in his pocket for the moment. He could not scrub floors and keep his eyes on loose bills at the same time ; he was not paid three dollars a week and obliged to pass every penny of it into the family exchequer for that ! Yet, it must be admitted that from the outset his mind dwelt by preference upon one side of the question, namely, that the money would probably never be missed, and that, even if it were, no one could guess where it had gone. The necessary inference is, that Tim's moral nature was not highly developed, for when once he had got to his feet, and had walked past Simon Barry without being found out, he was well on the road to regarding himself as the undisputed owner of the bill.

Whether the money would have been spent without retributory pangs of a tardy conscience, is a question that will never be answered, for Tim was destined to experience an unlooked-for check in the downward career so propitiously begun ; a check which occurred in this wise.

When, a few minutes later, the young transgressor had accomplished a hasty exit from the bank and found himself standing in the rain outside, he did not at once seek the seclusion of his own home, and for the very obvious reason that seclusion was not to be found there. Given a tenement of five rooms and a family of nine persons, including a sharp-eyed grandmother, there was little opportunity for a harassed mind to take counsel with itself, to say nothing of the difficul-

An Unlucky Windfall

ties in the way of that ocular gloating over his ill-gotten gains for which the boy's soul thirsted. He therefore bent his eager steps toward a certain region of wharves and warehouses, in the shadow of which were sundry flights of half-decayed wooden stairs. These led down to floating piers, especially secluded at low tide, where, at this hour of a rainy afternoon, he might hope to be unobserved.

Arrived at the foot of one of these flights, he stepped upon the slippery float and gazed cautiously about. There was not a soul in sight at the windows of the warehouses, nor along the narrow walk at their base, and the outlook into the mist-blurred harbor was quite cut off by the great black stern of a big freighter which lay across the mouth of the slip, some fifty yards distant. The rain had almost ceased, and there was a distinct brightening in the west, but the whole city lay between him and that. Somehow he did not want the sun to come out just yet, and lest it should surprise him, and also because he could not longer control his impatience, he pulled the bill from his pocket and spread it out in his hands, the better to study its ingratiating features.

At this juncture, for the first time in his life, Tim found himself compelled, by sudden stress of emotion, to sit down, and he did so, precipitately, upon a cold, oozy step of the stairway. Horrified, transfixed, he gazed at the appalling succession of cyphers following that figure 10 which had so appealed to his fancy, and, thanks to the laws touching compulsory education, he was scholar enough to perceive that the value of this unlikely bit of a bill which he held in his hands was nothing less than ten thousand dollars payable in the gold coin of the United States of America!

Tim sat for several seconds on that oozy step, vainly trying to grasp the enormity of the situation. Ten thousand dollars! He believed that was a million! He sprang to his feet, breathing hard. For one wild moment he thought of himself as a millionaire, and he raised his eyes to a giant warehouse, looming above him, while a strange, uncanny exultation possessed itself of his soul. Visions of splendor, undefined but bewildering, rose before his mental eye. They strongly resembled some of the scenes at a circus, —the recent sight of which he owed to Truxton's munificence,—and they were consequently strong in tinsel and fiery steeds.

And at this point in his meditations, it must be recorded in justice to Tim, his hitherto dormant conscience turned in its sleep. It might be no great harm to steal ten dollars from an institution that was rolling in riches, but—to steal ten thousand dollars! No—the boy that did that would undoubtedly go to hell! He glanced at the dark water lapping the slimy green piles of the wharf. It was dead-low tide and the shadows were horribly black in under there. He shuddered as if those inky depths had been the very waters of the Styx.

At this crucial moment the sun came out, and, striking across the windows of a certain grim warehouse over yonder, sent a piercing, blinding ray of light straight into the boy's eyes. He hastily stuffed the note into his pocket and, climbing the slippery steps with all celerity, he started on a run for the Pilgrim Savings Bank.

He would bang on the door, he told himself as he sped along the great business thoroughfare; he would bang on the door until old Barry opened it, and then he would say he had forgotten something —he did not know what, for indeed Tim's possessions were not numerous enough to give much scope to his imagination in that direction. And while he was yet cudgelling his brain on this point the sight of a policeman at one of the crossings stayed his step. It would never do to have a "cop" ask him what was his hurry; that would assuredly have been the end of Tim! But his mental processes were only accelerated, as he walked on at a more moderate speed.

Yes, he would say he had forgotten something, and then, somewhere in the neighborhood of the paying-teller's desk, he would drop that piece of paper, and let it take its chances.

And presently he stood before the heavy door, and he banged upon it until his knuckles were bruised, and he kicked it till his toes ached, and the great door opposed itself to him, immovable, inexorable as Fate. And Tim knew that Simon Barry had gone home, and that that door was closed to him as fast and firm as ever the door of Paradise was closed to a sinner.

For two hours Tim sat on the step, hoping, with but a faint and failing hope, that Simon Barry might still appear; and when, at last, the boy got to his feet, and walked away, it was with a heavy heart and a harassed brow. Tim had learned the great lesson, though he could not have put it into words, that the exercise of free-will is one thing, and its consequences another.

CHAPTER XIV.

FOREST WAYS.

TRUXTON, meanwhile, all unconscious of the graver issues involved in Tim's moral aberration, was inclined to consider his telegram and the proposition contained therein paramount to every other interest that life afforded. The telegram was from Shepleigh, who was off for the wilds of Maine, and it was written with the exuberant extravagance which characterized that native of the Golden State as often as he had a desired end in view. Indeed, it was a well-established fact that Shepleigh was as prodigal of words in a telegraphic communication as he was niggardly in his epistolary efforts.

The despatch in question stated with all explicitness that the Shepleighs, who, with a party of friends, were bound for a camping-out 'expedition, had that moment learned that Truxton's vacation coincided with their dates, and it further informed him that, by a unanimous vote, he had been elected a member of the party. Nor was anything left to his imagination in the way of trains or routes, or touching the necessities or superfluities of an outfit; so that, as the recipient noted, with amused appreciation, he who read might run ! How Truxton blessed his luck in running across young Caleb Ware the day before, when the latter was on his way to the station to join his sister and the Shepleighs !

The two young men had compared notes as to their prospective outings, and Truxton could imagine the deliberateness of the cogitations on Caleb's part which had not flowered into speech on the subject until after he had slept upon it.

Truxton had been trained in boyhood to camp-life ; there had been no closer bond of sympathy between himself and his father than their common love of sport, their common skill in woodcraft. It was a taste, indeed, which had had but scant gratification since his father's death, but that it had lost none of its charm would have been evident in the quickening of the pulse with which he had listened to Caleb's account of his prospects, even before he knew anything of the composition of the party.

Is it any wonder, then, that Truxton accomplished the impossible that afternoon? That, with but four hours to spare, he got his tenement-house business wound up, his valise packed, and his rifle and shot-gun cleaned? That he found time to explain his change of plan with bewildering brevity to his aunt, and to notify Stone and

Rathbone of his defection? And, as a result of this output of executive ability, he presently found himself comfortably ensconced in the east-bound night-train, wrapped in that sense of peace and satisfaction which descends upon the good traveller in the midst of the rushing and roaring, the jolting and jarring, the fitful glares and the all-devouring gloom of a midnight passage across country.

It seemed to him as if he were leaving all relation with his every-day life behind him as completely as the bald facts of it. The bank was behind him, with Flynn and the cash-box and the incalculable depositor; Launcelot Avenue was gone, and Broad Street, the Widow O'Toole and Mattie Tripe. Even Aunt Lucretia was becoming dim, receding with her dignities and eccentricities and the very dragon on the front door into a region as remote to his thoughts as that which they had occupied a few years ago when all the period of his youth and all the waves of the Atlantic had washed between.

And, as the past receded, as the train went rushing and roaring through the night, the present took on a curiously picturesque interest, and there arose within him an exultant feeling that all the forces of civilization were on his side. Electricity had summoned him, steam was bearing him onward; in the interval the telephone had played its part, and the electric car; and what a wonderful system that was by which a slip of paper signed with the modest name of Frank Truxton could be exchanged at a moment's notice for sundry government obligations of assorted values bearing the signature of the Treasurer of the United States of America ! He paused with a half-humorous relish upon the thought that to all intents and purposes the one signature was as valid as the other ! Then, as the locomotive gave a prolonged shriek which seemed but to accelerate the speed, he once more gave himself up to the joy of rushing forward, the noisier, the rougher the progress, the more convincing it seemed.

Truxton purposely kept his mind fixed upon the tangible, indisputable means which were so squarely within his grasp ; he would not let his thoughts leap forward to the end. That would be too risky—Fate might resent it ! And because a subtle aroma of hope and joy had touched his spirit, which yet he would not trace to its source, it was given him on that night of jolts and noises, of air heavy with cinders and vocal from time to time with the wails of a too youthful passenger— on just this night of all nights it was given him to perceive the poetry of common things as he had never done before. And if, from time to time, his thoughts approached the limit which they had so long recognized and deferred to, they never once overstepped it. One of these days, perhaps—one of these days—but meanwhile how the train banged and roared ! He could have hugged that splendid old engine in sheer gratitude and exultation.

Nor did he ever entirely forget the vigorous steed of steam when, in the days that followed, he strolled through lonely " tote-roads," or glided to the stroke of the paddle down shallow streams or across the peaceful bosom of a forest lake.

" I don't suppose we should know how lovely this was," he said one day to Ruth, " if we hadn't roared and racketed to get here."

It was their third day in camp, but to Truxton it was the beginning of everything, for Ruth was reclining for the first time in the bow of his canoe, dreamily watching the dip of his paddle and all the delicate stirring of the quiet waters that broke and dimpled, lapped and whispered to the stroke.

" Did we racket and roar ? " she asked ; " I don't believe I remember."

" Oh, yes ; we racketed and roared. If we had not we should not care so much about this."

" You think not ? "

" Don't you ? "

" I'm afraid somebody will have to do my thinking for me. I can't get beyond the ripple your paddle makes. Is there anything else going on in all the world, I wonder ? "

" Yes ; there's a shadow passing across that dear old hump of a mountain behind you. Wait ! " and Truxton turned the canoe that Ruth might look into the deep, brooding heart of the mountain.

"Thank you," she murmured, lazily. "If this were to go on forever we should forget how to turn our heads."

"No harm, that, since we should not need to," Truxton declared with conviction.

He liked the desultoriness of the talk; it seemed to keep things just where they were, despite the fact that the canoe itself was gradually making for the shore. As they drew near the beach, beyond which the camp-fire was burning and the tents gleaming white among the trees, a shot resounded with the startling suddenness which is so marked a characteristic of firearms!

"How rude!" Ruth exclaimed. The lively resentment of her tone roused an answering feeling in the oarsman's mind.

"It's Shepleigh, shooting at a sand-peep— with a rifle, too, the savage! Try again, Will," he sang out, as the canoe glided nearer the shore; "he does n't seem to take your point!" And indeed the peep had continued tilting about on the edge of the water some sixty yards away, quite unconcerned with the roaring echoes that answered to his enemy's shot.

"I was only signalling for supper," Shepleigh retorted; "I thought I would invite Mr. Peep to join us. The stew's done, and you 're the last in."

"Here; let me have it," said Harkness Dole, who had sauntered up behind Shepleigh. Truxton's canoe was close in shore as Dole raised the gun to his shoulder, and, with a cursory glance along the barrel, fired. A scattering wisp of feathers floated through the air and sank into the tiny wavelets of the little beach.

"Pretty shot!" Shepleigh cried.

"Oh," Ruth gasped; "I wish he had n't!"

A curious feeling of indignation seized upon Truxton and, as he beached his canoe and gave Ruth a hand to shore, he purposely turned his back upon the two men.

"Here, Truxton," Dole called, reloading the rifle and running his thumb along the shining barrel; "there's a chance for you. Will you try it?" and he nodded his head toward another tiny beach where another sand-peep was running up and down and fluttering its soft feathers with the eager animation of its kind.

"Thanks," said Truxton, curtly; "I should rather fire at something nearer my own size."

Dole shrugged his shoulders.

"You would probably have a better chance of hitting it," he answered, composedly.

"Right you are!" Truxton agreed, his good temper getting the better of him. And in truth he was too good a shot, though his fellow-campers did not know it, to mind the thrust particularly.

"Please don't, Harkness!" Ruth begged; for Dole had raised the rifle for another shot.

"Why not?" he queried; but he lowered the gun and transferred his attention to Ruth. She was standing beside him, watching the glancing light on the soft plumage.

"They are so happy," she said; "and so small! It seems like murder!"

"More so than shooting partridges?"

"Of course! We eat the partridges."

"Thou shalt not commit murder," Dole declaimed, "unless for thine own carnal profit. See the revised edition of the Ten Commandments."

"Don't be too logical," Shepleigh cried, "or the girls will all turn vegetarians, and won't allow the rest of us to have any biscuit!"

"Oh, Ruth won't be vindictive," Dole replied, with easy concession; "because she knows she is in the right of it."

"And you will never shoot another peep?" Ruth asked, as they turned to stroll up the beach to their supper. Truxton, walking behind with Shepleigh, could see Dole's face as he looked into Ruth's earnest, half-beseeching, half-challenging eyes.

"Never," he answered, simply.

"Mr. Partridge and Mr. Rabbit were more polite than Mr. Peep when I invited them to supper," Shepleigh remarked, in modest reference to his own prowess, as he handed Ruth a tin plate filled with savory morsels of game.

"I wonder who will get the muskrat," Jim Foxborough speculated, gravely, fishing about in the kettle as if in anxious search.

"The what?" cried his sister Daisy, with gratifying consternation.

Curiously enough, Miss Daisy did not look quite so "woodsy" here, in the heart of the forest, as she had done at the Shepleigh dinner-party. To Truxton's thinking, at least, it was Ruth who seemed most naturally at home among the green shadows and the sifting sunshine, it was Ruth's voice that seemed next of kin to the voices of nature. Yet Daisy Foxborough was, nevertheless, a very picturesque feature of a picturesque scene.

"The muskrat," her brother repeated, gravely. "They are delicious eating, Mrs. Shepleigh, but we only got one, and I am dreadfully afraid you ladies may miss it."

"Oh, no! I discovered it at once!" Mrs. Shepleigh retorted, with gentle leisureliness. "They are considered a great delicacy in Virginia, where I used to visit."

Clearly, Mrs. Shepleigh's wits did not partake of the slowness of her speech.

"O Clara! I wish Jim were your brother!" Daisy exclaimed; "he needs somebody to deal with him, and I never arrive in time."

"That is because you start too soon," was the reply; and Mrs. Shepleigh leaned back among the roots of a big pine-tree, a very comfortable throne, which she had appropriated by virtue of her dignity as chaperone.

Mrs. Shepleigh was the only member of the

company whose function was purely passive. A chaperone, she was wont to explain, is a person who lives and lets live. It is her first duty to set an example of doing as you please. The chaperone in question never took a hand in the camp work, and this in itself gave her an unique position, for the camp was nothing if not coöperative. If Dan Warnick, the sole guide, performed rather more of the manual labor than anyone else, it was because his muscles were in better training and his endurance greater.

Dan was a fine, stalwart young fellow who could not be said to despise social distinctions, since he was absolutely unaware of their existence. His respect for his fellow-workers was founded upon their strength in felling trees and handling gunny-bags, their prowess with rod and gun; his regard for Ruth and Daisy grew as the skill increased with which they could lay a carefully thatched bed of fir-branches, or ply the stern paddle of a canoe. And yet there was an inconsistent deference in his treatment of Mrs. Shepleigh, the only unblushing idler of the company, which went to show that the most primitive nature has its little involutions and obscurities.

All had a hand in the cooking, and the results, if sometimes problematical, never lacked that dramatic interest of which Jim Foxborough had just tried to take undue advantage. The composition of the stew, especially, was left largely to chance, each member of the company contributing whatever seemed to him desirable. At the same time, individual aptitudes received prompt recognition. To Caleb Ware, the acknowledged champion of the rod, was further conceded supremacy in the frying of trout; Shepleigh knew the secret of mixing biscuit, his huge hands possessing a lightness of touch which the girls themselves could not rival; while Harkness Dole, squatting, with a sardonic grin, before the scorching embers, could toss a flapjack higher, and catch it more deftly than even Truxton, who had indulged in modest visions of distinguishing himself in that line. In fact, Dole had an exasperating way of doing things better than anyone else; he had even developed an uncanny gift, that seemed to partake of the nature of second-sight, in regard to the weather.

"There's my thunder-storm," he remarked, as he skillfully conveyed a flapjack of enormous dimensions from the frying-pan to a plate which Daisy held expectant; and, at the word, a low muttering became audible, apparently somewhere in the depths of the forest behind them.

"Harkness makes his prophecies so long in advance that we forget all about them unless they happen to come true!" It was Caleb Ware who broke through his accustomed taciturnity to cast discredit upon the prophet. Mrs. Shepleigh had promised to go out with him on the lake that evening, and here was Harkness spoiling everything with his uncalled-for thunder-storms!

Caleb liked Mrs. Shepleigh; she never talked too fast.

Darkness was gathering early, and the light from the camp-fire shone brighter. The melancholy voice of a loon was heard, close inshore, causing Shepleigh to seize a gun and hasten to the water's edge with intent to kill. But the loon, more wary than the peep, had taken alarm and vanished under water, only to reappear, with a derisive laugh, well out of range.

As Dole's last flapjack fulfilled its mission, the company rose to its feet and fell upon the dishes, while darkness thickened swiftly. A hoot-owl joined his lamentations to the weird derision of the loon, and Warnick, overcome by the melancholy suggestions of the hour, began a tuneful wail to the effect that he had "lost his wife and child, and never more had smiled, but still went roaming on from place to place."

"Oh, give us a rest, Dan!" cried Shepleigh; for that red-handed murderer of small game was easily lacerated in his feelings. "You never had a wife and child to lose; you know you did n't!"

"Me! I guess not!" was Dan's cheerful reply. Then, waxing confidential, he paused, stew-kettle in hand, to say, "We ain't a marrying lot, any of us. There 's my sister now; she 's a real smart girl, but I don't believe she ever *sot up with a feller* in her life."

At this juncture the rain began falling in big drops and the girls hastily took refuge in their tent, the generous dimensions of which were a tangible witness to the thoroughgoing character of Yankee chivalry; the ladies' quarters being at least twice as large as those devoted to the men, who outnumbered them two to one. Caleb and Jim proceeded to haul the canoes high up on the beach and turn them bottom upwards, while Dan and Truxton got a roaring fire started before the tent that should outlive any civilized thunderstorm. The main tent-ropes were tightened and the side-flies fastened taut to the pegs. Then, while Ruth and Daisy prepared the lime-juice toddy, an innocent beverage with which the company were in the habit of regaling themselves at convivial moments, Mrs. Shepleigh decreed that Dan was to give them the *Lumberman's Ditty*.

The young man, nothing loath, began promptly in a sonorous voice, remarkably melodious and well-modulated, considering its source:

> " A is for Axes you very well know,
>   B is the Boys that can use them also;
>   C is the Chopping which we put them in,
>   D is the Danger we ofttimes are in!"

Upon which the entire company, with a gusto which testified to appreciative familiarity, joined in the chorus:

> " For so merry, *oh*, so merry are we,
>   No mortals on earth are so merry as we!
>   Hi derry, hi derry, hi derry down,
>   Give a shanty-boy rum and there 's nothing goes
>   wrong!"

This chorus, even to its highly immoral ending was rendered with great spirit by all concerned, Shepleigh adding much to the effect by the vigor of his untuneful bellowing.

The rain had become a downpour, and before resuming his performance, Dan stepped outside and flung a huge birch-bark log on the fire, causing it to blaze up with unquenchable enthusiasm. As he came in, he gave himself a shake, which sent the drops flying in every direction, and, remarking that he would " as lief have a regular rain as a shower like that to last twenty-four hours," he flung himself down on the pine-boughs and devoted four more lines to the Echo, the Foreman, the Grindstone, and the Handle, respectively. And again the company joined with unabated ardor in the chorus.

" I wish you boys would smoke a little faster," Daisy begged ; " the mosquitoes have all come in out of the wet and we want a regular smudge ! " She had gathered herself together behind her brother, to the leeward of his pipe, and even Truxton was forced to admit that her black eyes, shining through the smoke in the fitful firelight, looked very like the eyes of some forest creature.

So the five men puffed and pulled with renewed zeal, while the abstemious Dan, who, despite his convivial chorus, neither smoked nor drank, forged his melodious way through the alphabet in praise of the lumberman's life. All irregularities of rhyme and metre were merged in the swing and rhythm of his performance, and the imagination was constantly stimulated by the range and variety of images suggested.

The fourth verse was a special favorite by reason of the catholic liberality with which it touched upon nature, domestic industry, ornithology, and woodcraft.

> " M is the Moss that we find in our camps,
> N is the Needle that mended our pants;
> O is the Owl that hooted at night,
> P is the Pine that we always *fall right!*"

Only at the end does the poet's invention fail, and after stating in the previous verse that he has " sung all he is going to sing," he frankly admits the quandary and substitutes sentiment for technicalities, declaring :

" There are three more letters I can't bring in rhyme,
And if you will have me, pray tell me in time,
For the cars they are going, the whistle doth blow,
So fare ye well, darling, for I must go too!"

and once more the chorus rose with renewed energy, and,

> " Hi derry, hi derry, hi derry down,"

they shouted, till the sound of the rain on the tent was lost, and the fire blazed with the noiselessness, though not with the fixedness, of a pictured flame. The pungent odor of the fir-branches that formed the floor of the tent penetrated the "smudge" of tobacco smoke, and the sense of the forest grew so near and intimate that one could all but feel the breath of it on the cheek.

As the chorus came to an end, with a snap like a whip-lash—which feature of the performance was Jim Foxborough's specialty—they could again hear the patter of the rain, but it was somewhat gentler than before.

"Now the *Canoe-Song*, Mrs. Shepleigh."

It was Harkness Dole who asked it. He was leaning back in the shadow where the firelight which played upon the other faces did not reach his. Truxton felt, somehow, as if he had taken that position with malice prepense; it gave him an advantage. A supposition on Truxton's part which, be it observed, showed that he had allowed his imagination to get the better of him.

Mrs. Shepleigh, who had been leaning against her husband's broad shoulder, sat forward a little, and, clasping her hands on her knees, she sang the song with much sweetness and simplicity, and with a gentle dreaminess of attitude and inflection. As she sang, the rain on the canvas, growing ever gentler, tapped a rhythmic accompaniment to the lilt of words and music:

"They launched their light birch on the twilight lake,—
   Oh, was it a lake, or was it a dream?
 As they glided away they could see in their wake
   The light of the camp-fire ruddily gleam.

"The dip of the paddle was all they heard,
    Save the whispering waves on the slender prow,
And each in the silence was strangely stirred
    By a fancy which neither had cared to avow.

"In the deepening twilight the stars came out,
    And down in the water they sparkled and shone,
So bright and so near, there could be no doubt
    'T were easy to gather them, one by one.

"But something withheld them, they did not dip
    For the stars that sparkled so bright and near,
And sweet though the fancy they let it slip,
    And floating along they forgot to steer;

"Till at last their bark touched the shelving shore,
    No matter how loath they might be to awake,
The fancy was flown and the dream was o'er,
    And they left the stars in the shimmering lake!"

"It's too long, I know," Mrs. Shepleigh admitted, as she sank back into an easier posture; "but it would never do to leave them out on the lake. They were just the kind of people to get drowned."

"Awful duffer, the fellow was," declared Jim Foxborough; "might have seen, with half an eye, that she was ready to tumble!"

"Not so sure of that," Shepleigh demurred, with the wisdom of experience. "A fellow never feels sure."

"Perhaps he spoke when they got ashore," Caleb suggested. "A canoe's a ticklish place to get excited in!"

There was a general laugh at this matter-of-fact view of the subtleties of the situation.

"No, he never spoke," said Harkness Dole, in a tone of quiet authority.

"More fool he," Jim retorted.

"What do you say, Truxton?" asked Shepleigh. "Did he ever speak?"

"I rather think that is something that nobody knows but the man who wrote the verses."

"Mr. Dole thinks he knows," said Daisy, with mischievous intent. "Did you write the poem, Mr. Dole?" and she twinkled across at him as she had done on a previous occasion when truth in the abstract was the subject of her investigations.

Truth in the concrete seemed to fare no better, for Dole, replying, "Yes; that, and *Go Not, Happy Day*, are considered my most felicitous effusions," strolled forth into the night and the forest dripping with moisture and pungent odors.

"I believe he did write it," said Mrs. Shepleigh; "though I never thought of it before. It was he who gave me the song last spring."

"Do you suppose he did, Ruth?" Daisy asked. "You know him better than the rest of us do."

"I've no idea," said Ruth. "His things are usually better than that."

"Is there anything the white robin can't do?" asked Truxton, a few minutes later, as they stood on the beach, about to launch the canoes for an evening paddle. The stars were coming out among the clouds and, as Caleb had demonstrated, the canoes afforded the only dry foothold outside the tents.

"Yes," Ruth answered, with a thoughtful smile. "He can't be like other people."

"I suppose that is because he is a white one!"

"I don't think it was very 'white' of him to leave me in the lurch!" she laughed. "I knew by the way he went tramping over those sopping leaves into the woods that he had forgotten all about having asked me to go out this evening!"

"You can't expect me to resent that," was Truxton's daring rejoinder, "since I am to be the gainer!"—the temerity of which statement consisted in the fact that Ruth had not yet accepted him as substitute. "There's really nobody left, you know," he urged, growing a little anxious; "for Jim's gone for a bath, and the others are all paired off."

"I was thinking of paddling my own canoe," Ruth demurred. "That seems so much more appropriate for a deserted damsel."

"Then won't you take me as passenger?"

"Well, yes, I might," she answered, with a properly judicial hesitation; "though I am afraid it will rather destroy the effect."

The little fleet made a picture as it floated for a moment in the ruddy glow from the camp-fires. Then, as the birches stole apart in the darkness, the tiny light of a candle flickered at each prow, and dropped a thin, golden ray into the water, grown still as any mirror.

Above the woods, where the faithless Harkness had disappeared, a black remnant of the receding storm hung tattered and shorn of its menace, and somewhere over there a hoot-owl screamed. From Caleb Ware's canoe, which was not far away, came Clara Shepleigh's voice from time to time, singing snatches of the *Canoe-Song:*

"And down in the water they sparkled and shone,
 So bright and so near, there could be no doubt
 'T were easy to gather them, one by one."

And, after all, the paddle, whose gentle dip kept time with the music, was in Truxton's hands, for Ruth had let him have his way.

CHAPTER XV.

A GOOD SHOT.

TRUXTON'S sentiments towards Harkness Dole were becoming somewhat mixed; and, indeed, aside from any consideration of conflicting interests, there was that in the elder man's personality which rarely failed to stimulate curiosity. Though the familiar companion of most of the party, he was something of a puzzle to all.

In his public life Dole was an adroit politician, and events were apt to demonstrate that he belonged to the more beneficent order of the species. He sometimes perplexed his followers, yet he never deceived them, and, in spite of this reversal of the ordinary process, he usually led them to successful issues. This Truxton had noted, for, from the first evening of their acquaintance, he had found himself moved to make a study of a career which was plainly so interesting to Ruth. He had not only watched Dole's movements and utterances of the moment, but he had talked of him with men who were better posted than himself; to such good purpose, indeed, that he was within an ace of becoming interested in the general subject of politics, which he had hitherto been disposed to regard with a not altogether respectful indifference. As a result of these investigations Truxton had conceived so high an opinion of Harkness Dole's ability and character that he would have been almost as ready as Ruth to make a hero of him, had he been as unconscious as she of one phase of the situation.

And indeed if Ruth alone, of all the company, had reason to think that she really knew her cousin, it was precisely because of this belief that she was the more liable to a misapprehension of his attitude toward herself. Whether or not it was true, as Truxton suspected, that the old affection and good-comradeship, dating from her nursery days, had, in Dole, taken on a warmer, more exacting character, it is at least certain that no such suspicion had ever dawned upon her mind. And the illusion on her part, if illusion it was, was greatly encouraged by her cousin's cavalier treatment of her from time to time.

To Ruth's view, his desertion of her on the evening of the thunder-storm, and similar instances of absence of mind—or absence of manners, as Daisy Foxborough was inclined to consider it—were the prerogative of a friend and comrade. Yet, while she never thought of resenting these lapses and liberties, they were, on the other hand, quite incompatible with her notions of a lover—a branch of human lore in which, by the way, Miss Ruth Ware had not been without personal experience.

She had been told, years ago, that Harkness Dole would never marry, and she had accepted the current impression that he had once wished very ardently to do so. That was before her day, for he was thirteen years her senior. If that impression was a baseless one,—and one is constrained to discuss this matter in a purely hypothetical vein—the fact at least was well established in the family records, that the Harkness branch of the Dole family had, on general principles, better come to an end in this its last and best representative.

It would hardly be fair to a man of so much reserve as Harkness Dole, to narrate the bald facts touching three successive generations of his race, an unflinching recognition of which had induced the stand he had taken, but Ruth knew enough of the difficulties and denials which had confronted him from boyhood up, to give her a very fair understanding of his character, however she might misconstrue his sentiments.

All this, of course, Truxton could not know, and he was experiencing the discomfort of regarding as a rival a man whom he was strongly inclined to believe a better fellow than himself. Yet he was of too sanguine a temperament to lose heart at this stage of the game.

Although he did not for a moment suppose that Harkness Dole's defection on the evening of the thunder-storm was any indication of indifference, though the very puzzle of it was in itself disquieting, the fact nevertheless remained, that it was he, Frank Truxton, who had had the extreme felicity of floating with Ruth for an hour beneath the stars, while the camp-fire beckoned red across the water, and the fragrance of the pine-woods came and went. Sometimes a loon wailed in the shadow, sometimes Daisy Foxborough's gay laugh mingled with the hearty bass of Shepleigh's, sometimes it grew so still that the lisp of the water under the prow was distinctly audible. And, when Ruth spoke, there was that in the manner of her speech which convinced him that she was as well content as he; that, whatever her sentiments might be toward her cousin, she found satisfaction, for the moment at least, in the society of her new friend.

And so it had been on other occasions when chance had thrown them together. They had not talked over much, they had scarcely alluded to the special interests which had first drawn them together; all that was apparently as remote to Ruth's mind as to his. But they had fallen in with one another's mood so naturally and harmoniously, that, in spite of Harkness Dole, in spite of his own native modesty, Truxton had sometimes made bold to wonder whether to Ruth, too, there were not a subtly persuasive charm in their mutual intercourse. Could it be that she did not know that he loved her? He had never been on his guard as Harkness Dole invariably was, he had never practised any abnormal self-restraint. If he had not given utterance to his feelings, it was because he recognized the inherent fitness of things, because he did not think the time had come for laying overt claim to her regard. One of these days, one of these days! And meanwhile she must know, she must at least divine, the truth, and she suffered him to be happy. She was surely too intelligent to mistake him, to miss the truth he was at so little pains to conceal, and she was too sincere, too compassionate, to prepare for him a needless pain and humiliation. The girl to whom the poor and the lowly turned instinctively for protection, the girl who carried consolation to Mattie Tripe and sympathetic understanding to the Widow O'Toole, such a girl would never deal wantonly with the man who loved her.

And so it was, that even the dread of Harkness Dole could not long embitter the joy of the moment, and that, during those days, was born, in the odor of the pine-forest, a power over Frank Truxton to which he was profoundly susceptible ever after.

They had struck camp at dawn the following morning, and the little fleet, heavily loaded with the camp outfit, had pursued its way down the broad outlet of the lake to a new camping-ground.

Here, on the bank of the river, just below a dashing little waterfall around which they had been obliged to " carry," and in convenient neighborhood to a spring of ambrosial purity and coolness, a clearing had been made among the young birches, the tents were spread, and fir-branches laid. When, thanks to a crackling fire of birchwood, an excellent stew had got itself prepared for the workers and subsequently consumed, Harkness Dole had invited Truxton to go with him for a tramp after bears and porcupines. Truxton, who had always had a taste for bearding his lion, hailed with joy this opportunity, not of shooting problematical bears, but of tracking the mind of Harkness Dole to its ultimate lair.

They crossed the river on stepping-stones, a few rods above the falls, and here, coming upon an old " tote-road," they pursued their way up a steep incline. When, owing to the impeding growth of young wood, the road narrowed or disappeared altogether, Truxton fell behind.

As he trudged along, rifle in hand, he glanced with interest from time to time at the tall, wiry figure, advancing, with bent head and steady gait, unhindered by the underbrush, and bending young saplings aside with the butt of his rifle. Truxton carried his own gun over his shoulder and secretly hoped he might have a chance to use it; for when a man is a good shot it is too much to demand that he should be averse to having the fact known.

They tramped along for a couple of miles, till the road brought them out on a clearing where there were deer-tracks; and here they paused to take their bearings.

"Pity it's the off season," Dole remarked. "I believe we could follow that fellow up," and he pointed to fresh tracks disappearing into the woods at the right.

"Perhaps we could get a look at him as it is," Truxton suggested. "That's half the battle. I sometimes think," he added, "that one might get almost as much satisfaction out of a kodak as out of a gun. The shot's the main thing."

"Depends on which of the two you handle best," Dole rejoined, coolly. "For my part, I like to bag my game."

"I should think you might usually succeed in doing it, judging by your shot last evening."

"There was not anything left to bag on that occasion," Dole answered, drily. "And I am ready to admit that there's not much good in knocking things to pieces just to show how smart you are! You and Ruth had better sense."

Truxton felt himself flush in an exasperating manner.

"Do you suppose," he asked by way of diversion, "that we shall remember that old stump that we came out by when we get back here, or will a whole regiment of them spring up to rattle us?"

"No harm in barking a tree, but I should n't

wonder if we came back by the river. Perhaps these tracks will lead to it."

The weather was unseasonably warm, and Truxton had been glad to get the breeze that came across the clearing. Dole, on the other hand, looked as cool as when they started.

They followed the tracks into the woods, where they had to fight their way for a few rods through a tangled undergrowth, and then they emerged upon an open " tote-road " leading at right angles with the direction they had taken. The tracks went down-hill and here they could walk abreast. They did so, talking, in a low tone of voice, though they had little hope of anything turning up here, save partridges and rabbits.

" I fancy," Truxton remarked, " that it is your propensity for hitting things you aim at that makes such a good politician of you; " and he glanced over his shoulder to see whether the observation was well received.

" Possibly," Dole replied ; but his imperturbable countenance betrayed no sentiment either of pleasure or displeasure.

" I 'll give it to him square between the eyes!" Truxton thought to himself. Then, " I suppose you rather lead among the younger men of the State."

" I suppose so."

" I never took much stock in politics until I began looking up your record," Truxton added, composedly.

"No?" and this time Dole turned and glanced at his persistent interlocutor. Perhaps it struck him that it was about time to turn the tables. "I have been thinking, now that I know you better," he said, with a critical frown, "that you have some qualifications for the game yourself."

"I?"

"Yes; you. In the first place, you 've got considerable sense. Then—you get the hang of people quickly, and—you never sulk."

Truxton, who had listened respectfully up to this point, gave a short laugh.

"All the domestic virtues," he exclaimed. "I had n't thought of them as essentials!"

"No; I presume not. But a politician who has good sense, good perceptions, and good humor —and one quality besides—is fairly well equipped. How thick those bunch-berries are!"

"And what is the fourth qualification?"

"I 'll wait till I find out whether you 've got it before I tell you."

"And how do you propose to find out?"

"Oh, that 's my business—as a politician, if you will—to find out!"

"Has any politician ever found you out?"

"Perhaps not. That may be what gives me a pull over them," and there was something almost confidential in the side-glance he gave his companion. But he quickly disowned it by an abrupt change of subject. "Is n't that falling water that we hear?" he asked.

"Sounds like it. Dan said there were some bigger falls farther down the stream."

Presently Dole spoke again, as if under cover of the noise which was gradually increasing. And Truxton, on his part, listened with a curious feeling that the sound of the rushing waters covered any self-consciousness he might otherwise have betrayed.

"There's one other thing you've got," Dole was saying, "which would not necessarily make you more successful, but it might possibly make you more useful—if you did n't run it into the ground."

"And that is?"

"Ruth says that you have a notion of making things better. You would find that idea open up tremendously if you once got hold of the wheels."

Most persons listened respectfully to Harkness Dole when he chanced to be in earnest, and Truxton found himself doing so on this occasion, though from anyone else such a calm analysis of his own personal character would have struck him as grotesque.

"Pity there should be any doubt about that other qualification," he found himself replying, quite seriously. "It would n't be half bad to be both successful and useful,—in any walk of life. You must have found that out before this."

Dole's face became a thought more non-committal than usual, and, not being the kind of man to shout, his voice was only just audible above the steadily increasing roar of the falls as he said, "That's as you may look at it."

A moment more and they could see the fall showing white among the trees, and as they approached the bank the spray touched their faces. The deer-tracks led on down-stream, and, after an appreciative consideration of the fine, free leap of the river, and of the churning rapids below, Truxton proposed keeping up the pursuit.

"Go ahead," said Dole, and this time he was forced to shout, for the roar of the water was quite deafening. "I'm going to stay here and see if I can't make the game come to me."

The tracks stopped at the bank of the river, which was very shallow here where it had room to spread itself out, and, though the shore was somewhat trampled, as if the animal had paused to drink, there was no sign of his having turned back. He had probably been startled by their voices and had crossed the stream before they reached it. It would have been pretty to see the creature drink here in this natural fastness.

The fall was thundering away in fine shape fifty yards up the glen and the wide shallow below was still flecked with foam as the water hurried among the rocks. Truxton stepped across from rock to rock to the other shore, which proved to be but the pebbly edge of the river-bed left dry by the summer's drought, and, where the rocky bottom ceased, the woods pressed close. He felt that the deer might be in there almost anywhere, gazing, with big, mild eyes, at the two-legged intruder; but he could find no trace of him, nor did the woods offer any pathway.

Truxton forced a passage through a thicket of alders and birches and pressed on against an all but impenetrable tangle. He knew he could find his way back by following the sound of the waters, and he knew, too, that he should not be led far astray in the midst of such obstacles as these. More than once he found himself confronted by a gigantic boulder whose towering, precipitous sides presented an insurmountable barrier. He made it a point of honor to fight his way about the base. Once he stepped upon the huge trunk of a prostrate tree which yielded beneath his weight, so that he came crashing through into a mush of rotten bark and fibre. He enjoyed this hand-to-hand tussle with a very uncompromising Nature, and he kept it up, quite for its own sake, having long since given up his deer. Now and then, when he paused for breath, strange noises struck his ear and roused a momentary curiosity; but, being versed in woodcraft, he was well aware that no man has ever learned the secret of all the forest tongues, their whisperings and their mutterings, nor of the strange stirrings of the breath, the pulsing in the veins, of the untrodden wilderness.

His wrestling-bout had lasted close upon half an hour, yet he knew by the sound of the falls that he had made but little progress. As he came to the edge of the woods, only a few rods farther down-stream than he had entered them, he could see Harkness Dole, gun in hand, pacing up and down the stony shore. Dole did not seem to be watching for him, nor to be on the lookout for game.

Truxton paused a moment before showing himself; the sight of the solitary man pacing there interested him. Yet there was nothing in his face or bearing different from his usual aspect. There were the lines of quiet concentration, that was the look of withdrawal from external interests, which always marked his countenance when in repose. Here was the same nonchalance of bearing which always characterized him—which scarcely left him when paddling with all his strength and skill against the rapids, which was never more complete than when he was about to pull the trigger. For a man so highly organized, so complicated, there was a curious consistency in his outward manifestation.

Truxton stepped out of his covert of boughs, and at the same moment Dole flung himself down on a sun-baked space among the rocks, where moss and grass were making a praiseworthy effort to flourish. He leaned his elbow in the moss, and, resting his head in his hand, pulled his hat over his eyes. His legs were stretched at full length before him.

By this time Truxton was exactly opposite him across the stream, which was perhaps twenty yards wide at that point. As he paused, to choose the best crossing, his eye was caught by a something moving in the sparse grass close to Dole's elbow. He shouted, but his voice did not carry against the roar of the falls and the chatter of the rapids, and, before he could take a step forward, the head of a snake had raised itself from the writhing coils, and he knew that in another instant the creature would strike.

A moment for reflection would perhaps have paralyzed him ; but his action was necessarily instantaneous. With a movement as involuntary as that which causes the eye to close in self-defence, Truxton raised his rifle and fired. Yet, in the inappreciable second's pause before the pulling of the trigger, he had aimed with a swift intensity of concentration which was better than deliberation, and he experienced no feeling of surprise when the creature dropped.

Roused by the shot, Harkness Dole drew himself together and glanced carelessly across the stream at Truxton, and then his eye was attracted, by a last convulsive movement, to the evil thing not two feet away. He sprang to his feet and took a step backward. The thing was motionless —a long, gleaming rope of olive-brown, with darker spots, terminating in a curious, horny appendage. The head was completely demolished.

Dole stood there, quietly measuring with his eye the distance between the two shores, while Truxton took it in long, splashing leaps. The younger man's face was white beneath the tan and his eyes shone with excitement.

"Pretty shot," Harkness Dole remarked, as Truxton came up; but his words were drowned in the roar of the falls.

"Shall we try following the river?" Truxton shouted; and he was amazed to find how much voice he had, for he knew that he was vibrating inwardly in great, disconcerting pulses. He started on, up-stream, with a curious desire to get away from something.

"Hold on! The rattle's yours!" Dole called.

Then, as Truxton pushed on up the river, Dole took out his jack-knife and carefully removed the rattle, which he dropped into his pocket. After which he glanced again across the river, and, drawing a long, low whistle, audible only to his own ears, started in pursuit of Truxton.

He caught up with him, nearly half a mile above the falls, where the silence struck the ear as something strange and unnatural, in spite of the crunching of their boots on the stony border of the river-bed.

"So that's the kind of shot you are!" Dole observed, as he came abreast of Truxton.

"When I'm in luck," Truxton laughed—for he had got himself quieted down by this time.

They walked on, side by side.

Presently: "What was the thing doing when you fired?" Dole asked.

"Doing? What do you suppose he was doing?

You don't suppose I should have fired under your nose if he had been asleep?"

"Then he was—roused?"

"Well, rather! He was up on his elbow, taking aim. Nasty-looking chap, too!"

"H'm! I don't suppose it would have been a pleasant mode of exit, and—I 'm sure I 'm much obliged to you. Here 's the rattle."

"Thanks!" and Truxton took it in his hand and examined it. "Queer-looking machine! First I ever saw!" Then, with a sudden revulsion of feeling, he tossed it into the river.

"Hullo! What did you do that for?" Dole queried.

"Gave me the *jim-jams!* Would you care to have it, though? I think we could fish it out again."

"Oh, no; and I think you are entitled to the *jim-jams.*"

Half an hour later, as they came in sight of the camp-fire, showing faint and dim across the river in the broad day, Harkness Dole laid his hand on his companion's arm—a sort of thing Truxton had never known him to do before—and said: "There 's nothing to prevent my telling you, now, what that fourth qualification is."

"All right; fire away!" said Truxton. "Perhaps it can be cultivated!"

"It looks as if it had been," Dole replied. "It is what, for want of a better name, we sometimes call—*nerve!*"

CHAPTER XVI.

OUT OF A CLEAR SKY.

AFTER such an exploit as this, we may well believe that Truxton became the hero of the hour. Harkness Dole had casually mentioned the circumstance in the course of supper-time, so casually, indeed, that it was some seconds before the true significance of the event was apprehended. The excitement which followed was what any well equipped reporter would term " unparalleled." If Truxton escaped decoration at the hands of Mrs. Shepleigh, if Daisy Foxborough did not crown him with bunchberries in lieu of the traditional laurel, it was due to his agitated protest, vigorously seconded by Dole himself. If the boys, Jim and Caleb, did not hoist him upon their shoulders and bear him in triumph about the somewhat restricted limits of the clearing, it was because he proved too untractable to submit to such honors. But the spirit of adulation was abroad no less, and found expression in toast after toast, couched in the most flattering language, and drunk in lime-juice toddy to the health of Truxton, of Harkness, of the snake, and again of Truxton, and of Truxton again. It is even recorded that on this occasion Shepleigh made his initial venture in verse.

After sitting silent, pipe in mouth, for at least fifteen minutes, exhibiting a stoic indifference to relay after relay of Dole's flapjacks that passed unheeded beneath his usually susceptible nose, his brow, the while, corrugated with lines indicating extreme mental concentration, this mighty son of Anak suddenly burst into song, and roared out a more or less impromptu tail-piece to the *Lumberman's Ditty*.

"X is for Truxton who shot the big snake!
Y's for the Way that he done took the cake!
Z is how Dizzy we all of us turn
When we think how he scotched that unmannerly worm!"

Then, while the entire camp broke forth into clamorous plaudits, Dan took up the chorus, unsupported by the other voices; and the backwoodsman, perceiving that he was about to pluck a bay-leaf of his own, grew extremely red in the face as he approached the last line, and boldly amended it to:

"Give Mr. Truxton a gun and there's nothing goes wrong!"

The "Mister" which the performer bumped up against to the destruction of rhythm and metre, was an unprecedented tribute on the part of Dan who, as a rule, religiously avoided that courtesy-title.

But most of all did Truxton value a word of Ruth's. She had stepped down the bank to the edge of the stream, where he found her on her knees, engaged in the ordinarily unpoetic occupation of rinsing dish-towels. A half-grown moon, riding high overhead, lit her hair, which was lightly stirred by the breeze, and the water sparkled with the swish of the snowy linen.

Truxton came and stood beside her, watching her deft motions and waiting for her to speak first. Presently she stood on her feet and looked in his face.

" I thought it was you," she said.

" What made you guess ? "

" I suppose I was thinking of you before you came up."

" That was good of you."

" I was thinking," she said, very seriously, " of the danger you were in this afternoon."

" I ? "

" Yes ; you risked—everything ! "

" Most persons would call it rather a foolhardy performance," Truxton demurred.

" Yes ; *if they did n't know !* " And that was the word of Ruth's that outweighed all the rest.

The memory of it dwelt in his mind that evening as they sat about the camp-fire, capping one another's yarns of phenomenal shots and hairbreadth escapes; he heard it in the voice, he felt it in the warm pressure of the hand with which she bade him good-night; if the truth must be known, it was repeating itself in the strange, intermittent silences of the forest half the night through. Somehow, whether from the exhilaration of a feat accomplished, of a danger escaped, or because of a certain look Ruth's face had had down there by the river with the moon overhead, he was suddenly possessed of a most audacious self-confidence. Nor did it leave him in the days that followed.

Harkness Dole contributed to it as much as anyone. A certain intimacy had sprung up between the two men which was, in itself, disarming to Truxton's suspicions, though he was far from drawing from it the highly flattering conclusions which must have been patent to an onlooker. He never dreamed that Dole had deliberately taken his measure, and indeed the circumstance, had he been informed of it, would not have possessed any special interest for him. In his opinion, there was little in his own character to repay investigation, and it would have struck him that a man like Harkness Dole might have been better employed than in the study of it. What Truxton did take in, however, with keen appreciation, was his newly acquired privileges in the way of easy intercourse with a man of the world of Dole's calibre; and the fact that these were shared by Ruth was not calculated to detract from their value.

The three were much together, and the more he saw of Ruth's relation with Dole, the more complete he felt their mutual understanding to be, the less apprehensive did he grow. They had been friends for years, he reasoned, and no harm had come of it. Ruth was twenty-five years old and might be credited with knowing her own mind, while Harkness Dole, a man of means and influence, could have nothing to gain by delay. It was a miracle that they should not long ago have discovered how peculiarly suited they were to one another, but then, it was a well established fact that people never did what was expected of them, and in this instance, at least, the perversity of Fate was all in his favor.

Meanwhile, was there ever anything so enchanting as this rough camp-life, or so becoming to all concerned? Far from making him indifferent to others, it appeared as if his love for Ruth had opened his eyes to a thousand admirable traits in her fellow-campers. Far from suffering from comparison, all the rest of the company seemed to shine by a reflected light which was quite deceptively illuminating. Daisy Foxborough's vivacity charmed him as it had never done before; the indolent grace with which Mrs. Shepleigh maintained that inviolable poise of hers impressed him as something singularly perfect; Shepleigh himself seemed vastly more interesting than he had ever found him at college. As for Dan, Truxton was so enamored, not only of his character, but of his situation in life, that he found himself speculating as to how Ruth would like it if he were to turn lumberman, and invite her to spend the rest of her existence camping out! Not a bad idea that! Always to have the breath of the pine-woods in your nostrils, the sound of running waters in your ears, to make friends with Nature, take one's joys and one's reverses at her hands!

"How long do you think you could be happy in the woods?" he asked her abruptly, one day.

"Forever!" she answered, without a moment's consideration.

It was within a day or two of his departure for the city, but he would not let the thought of that intrude itself. They were wandering down an old "tote-road" that seemed to be leading them into the deepest depths of the forest. The partridges were so tame that he declared he should have been ashamed to shoot them. He knew, too, that the larder was full, and that Ruth had no taste for slaughter; so he carried his gun carelessly.

They came to a small clearing that had had time to conceal its wounds. The sunny space was strewn with ferns and bunch-berries, tender green moss had covered the stumps and fallen logs; even the rocks were clothed with lichen. A hundred spicy fragrances mingled with the all-pervading aroma of the balsam. Over their heads, as they sat upon a mossy rock, a chipmunk scolded and protested, and in among the bushes the bright eyes of small birds peered inquisitively.

They had sat there several minutes, talking in the low tone that the woodland induces, when they were startled by a sudden gust of whirring wings close at hand, and a little covey of three or four partridges shot like brown shadows into the woods. The birds did not go far; Ruth and Truxton could hear them clucking and peeping to one another just within the tangle.

"Perhaps this is their own special game-preserve we have blundered into," said Ruth. "I believe they feed upon those insects making a cloud of themselves in the sun."

"More likely that the birds do their housekeeping here," Truxton ventured. "I think that must be all one family from the way they keep on talking together."

"I believe we could understand what they say," Ruth declared, "if only that chipmunk would be quiet. Hush, hush!" she cried, waving her handkerchief at the impudent fellow, who only chattered the louder.

"Nothing short of a gun-shot would bring that chap to terms," Truxton remarked, but he made no motion to act upon his own suggestion.

As if appreciative of this exercise of forbearance, the little fellow presently stopped his chatter, and with a whisk, not of his tail, but of his entire person, disappeared.

At that, a hush fell upon the forest, broken only

by low, leafy rustlings and an occasional flutter of wings; for it was high noon, and the birds were not conversationally inclined.

"I wonder what makes this so utterly heavenly," Truxton speculated, leaning back against the trunk of a tree and clasping his hands behind his head.

Ruth did not answer at once; she had picked one of the ferns that grew at the base of their rock, and was studying its delicate tracery.

"I think I know," she said, at last. "I think it is because it is all so shut in. One takes it just as it is, without reference to anything else. If there were an outlook somewhere it would not be so peaceful."

"But it ought to be more inspiring."

"Oh, yes! So it would! But inspiration is n't peace, and I think, just now, just this minute, peace is the best thing."

Her hat, a soft dark felt, lay upon her knees; she bent her head above it and tucked the long fern in under the ribbon, but absently, as if it did not matter. The sun which was behind them, shining full upon the bent head, brought out the warm, rich tints of the hair. But her face was in shadow.

Truxton never forgot that hour with Ruth in the sunny glade among the scents and sounds of the forest. In a certain sense it seemed to him, as he looked back upon it, to have been the high-water mark of his life; the hour when the still tide of peace rose highest. The tossing waves of emotion, the whistling winds of ambition might fling the waters far above that level, but never could the tranquil gathering of the flood rise higher.

And, if violent contrast best emphasizes the character of an impression, that, too, was not lacking; for, scarce an hour after the chipmunk ceased his chatter and Ruth spoke her little homily on peace, came the rudest shock Frank Truxton had ever experienced.

They were camping that day on the shores of an island-strewn lake in whose glassy depths mountains and forests stood on their heads, and flights of wild duck crossed the blue of an inverted sky. A half-mile beyond their camp was a long "carry" through the woods to a companion lake of similar attractions, and here for the first time in ten days they were destined to come in touch with the outer world.

Two strangers from the city with their guides came paddling across the lake and paused for a friendly greeting. They did not disembark, but they tossed a couple of newspapers ashore which were dated only three days back. Truxton picked up one of them and handed it to Ruth, who accepted it with but a half-hearted interest. She was sitting on a log close to the water's edge, where she was polishing knives after the idyllic fashion so highly esteemed in camp circles, namely, by driving them vigorously into the clean white sand at her feet. As she took the paper she glanced down the little table of contents headed: "This Morning's News," and Truxton, who was watching her face, simply because that was always the most profitable use to which he could put his eyes, saw her change countenance and hastily turn the sheet. He wondered whether she had had ill news.

Suddenly she sprang to her feet and looked him in the face.

"Come," she said; "there is something you must see—but not now, not here—come!" and she walked swiftly up the beach to the camp-fire.

All the company were still gathered on the shore watching the long, shining wake of the stranger canoes.

"Miss Ware! What is it?" Truxton asked, half under his breath. "Have you had bad news?"

"News!" she repeated; "news! It's not news! It's an abominable lie, and I must be the one to tell you!" Her voice fairly broke upon the words.

Then, recovering herself, she handed him the paper. He saw that she was perfectly white, but there was a look of utter scorn on her face which he could not have dreamed it capable of.

Truxton took the sheet, and it was his own name that seemed to start out at him like a sudden sword-thrust. And then, while Ruth stood beside him, erect and defiant, with sparkling eyes and blanched cheek, and the voices of the others, still standing on the beach, came, like echoes from a remote past, he read the sensational head-lines:

"FRANK TRUXTON STILL AMONG THE MISSING!"

"COULD BE BETTER SPARED THAN THE FUNDS WHICH VANISHED SIMULTANEOUSLY."

Below, under the chastening influence of small type, appeared the following more moderate statement:

"Although the bank-officials, from president to janitor, refuse to be interviewed, there can be little doubt of the true state of the case at the Pilgrim Savings Bank. The incident is a severe blow to all concerned, for the young man was very popular, and, although he was known to be somewhat involved in mining speculations, he still possessed the entire confidence of his associates. The natural inference of course must be that the defaulting clerk, unable to withstand the insidious madness of speculation, has adventured his initial step on the downward path in a wild effort to stem the tide of financial ruin!"

Truxton read this highly imaginative effort twice through before he raised his eyes from the paper. When at last he lifted his face there were new lines there. The boyish look had gone from his eyes, and his mouth was drawn and stern.

"And you read—all that?" he asked.

"Every word," she answered.

"How could you?"

"How could I?" He could see the color come back into her face, slowly at first, then deepening swiftly over cheek and brow; but she did not flinch. "Do you think," she said, and her eyes were clear and steady as they met his,— "do you think that if that lie had been spoken I should have closed my ears to shut it out?"

"I should rather you had," he answered, almost harshly. "Hideous things are not fit for you to see or hear."

"They are as fit for me as for you," she declared, and she held out her hand to him with a gesture that gave a thrilling significance to the simple word and act.

Truxton took in his the proffered hand and bent his head above it with as knightly an impulse as if his Yankee breeding had permitted him to raise it to his lips. Yet his face, when he lifted it, was scarcely less stern, and the inflection of his voice, though no longer harsh, was strenuous and deliberate, the voice of a man in whom feeling must be held in check by the need of action.

"When the stain is gone from my name,—if stains ever do go,"—he added bitterly, "I shall come and thank you for this."

"And now?"

"Now I am going," and he turned abruptly, and strode down the little incline to the beach.

Ruth saw him hand the paper to Shepleigh and

speak to Harkness Dole; and then there was a sudden commotion in the little flock of figures on the beach, and, while Shepleigh remained behind for a word with Dan whom he had summoned from the woods, all the others came up, with anxious, bewildered faces.

Fifteen minutes later a canoe was launched and Truxton and Dan were off, speeding across the quiet lake to the swift, strong stroke of the two paddles.

"Good-bye and good luck!" Shepleigh shouted once, with a fair show of good cheer, and Dan waved his hand in response. But Truxton neither stayed his stroke nor turned his head, though the canoe swerved as the stern paddle paused an instant.

An oppressive silence fell upon the little company, staring disconsolate after the tiny craft.

"Think they'll find a team anywhere?" Dole asked, at last.

"Doubt it," said Shepleigh. "Guess Frank will have to foot it to the stage from the other side of Round Pond. But he'll make it."

"Oh, yes; he'll make it, fast enough."

"Starts at six in the morning, does n't it?" Caleb asked.

"Yes; he'll have a bad night of it," and Shepleigh's kind face was scored with the most painful emotions.

"What did he say, Will, when you offered to go with him?" his wife asked.

"He did n't say much, but—he made his meaning clear!"

"Beastly business!" Jim Foxborough observed. "I don't wonder he felt bad."

"But everything will be all right when he gets there," his sister remarked, with cheerful confidence.

"He won't get there till Saturday noon," Shepleigh rejoined, shortly. "That 's a good while to spend on a red-hot gridiron!"

The canoe, meanwhile, had disappeared among the islands. No one thought of anything consoling to say, and with one accord the company turned and strolled aimlessly up to the camp.

"I shall start for home to-morrow," Dole remarked, as he and Shepleigh walked together up the path which the feet of the campers had already worn in the sparse grass. "You can spare me a canoe when Dan gets back, and I know the way."

"Good!" Shepleigh exclaimed, reviving somewhat under the prospect of action; "and, look here, Dole, you may as well send the team back for the rest of us. Then we can get out on Sunday, and be at home by Monday night. What do you say, girls? We don't want to loaf around here any longer."

The proposition met with unanimous approval.

Presently Dole said to Ruth: "You can just catch the gleam of the paddles over there beyond that rocky island. Come and see!" and they walked back to the shore.

At first they could not find the canoe, but then the eye was caught by a white flash that came and went at regular intervals. Ruth, in whose brain the pulse of the paddles still beat, noted that the stroke had not varied by a second since they started out. She stood, her hands clasped in front of her, gazing sadly across the shining waters. Harkness Dole looked down upon her intently, as he said, in a quiet, matter-of-fact voice: "You care very much, Ruth, do you not?"

Then Ruth, too absorbed in her own feeling to mind betraying it, too single-hearted for any personal disclaimer, said: "Yes; *I care very much.*"

CHAPTER XVII.

UNDER A CLOUD.

THE period which had passed so happily for Frank Truxton in the wilds of Maine had been a time of much anxiety and depression in the ranks of the good old Pilgrim Savings Bank. For a week past, deep gloom had held possession of the pilgrims, a gloom which no efforts of mural decorators could dispel, which yielded not to the perennial though unconscious humors of the depositor, a gloom which even Flynn himself made no effort to lighten.

The discovery of a shortage of ten thousand dollars in the cash was in itself a pretty serious matter, but that any member of the gang—and Frank Truxton of all others—should be under suspicion cast a well-nigh intolerable reflection upon the men as a body. One short week ago they would have been prepared to maintain, against all comers, the personal integrity of every man on the pay-roll of the Pilgrim Savings Bank. For seventy-five years the institution had been a great financial stronghold of the city, for seventy-five years its servants had regarded themselves and one another as sharing the invulnerability of the bank itself. And now all that was changed, and there was not a man among them who did not feel that the pilgrims as a body were under a cloud.

It is needless to say that they did not at once succumb to these mournful suggestions. When, on the Monday morning, Plummer, returning from his vacation, took over the custody of the cash-box, and made a rapid comparison of the figures noted on the packages of bills with Truxton's memorandum, the discrepancy caused him only a sensation of annoyance that he should have blundered. Aleck Plummer had little patience with inaccuracy in himself or others, and, never doubting that Truxton's more careful count had been the correct one, he merely concluded that vacations were demoralizing things.

It was not until the middle of the morning that he found time to verify his reckoning, and then the sentiment of annoyance was only transferred to Truxton's account. The books would show a clerical error on Truxton's part—that was all. But the task of going over the books devolved upon him, Aleck Plummer, and he was anything but pleased at the prospect. He mentioned to Mr. Smith, the vice-treasurer, that he had got to dig out an error of Truxton's to the tune of ten thousand dollars, upon which Mr. Smith replied, consolingly: "An easier error to track than ten cents would have been. Rand was a million out one day last week, but it did n't take him long to find it!"

When, by the middle of the afternoon, Plummer had failed to trace the presumable error, he was sufficiently uncomfortable about it to report to Mr. Smith at his residence. The latter was the more annoyed at the news because of the fact that his chief, Mr. Seymour, was sailing from New York for Bremen the following morning, so that the brunt of any difficulty which might arise would come upon the vice-treasurer.

"Deuced careless of Truxton!" he said. "We shall have to have him back. Do you know where he is gone?"

"There was some talk of his going to Nova Scotia with Rand and Stone when I went away. He will have left his address."

But when inquiry was made, the next morning, it was found that the Nova Scotia address had been cancelled, that the Monday morning mail had brought directions to hold his letters. A telegram was sent to Rand at Wolfville, but it elicited no information beyond the fact that Truxton had backed out at the last minute, and later in the day a messenger was despatched to Miss Vickery, who replied that her nephew had left no address. The affair began to look serious, and a special meeting of the directors was called to consider the proper course of action. A detective was quietly put on the case, and the missing clerk was traced to the St. John's Express. Then the fatal word "Canada" got itself insinuated among the speculations of the pilgrims, and each man became vociferous in asseverations of Truxton's being "all right." Before that, they had scorned to make declarations in his favor. To call a man innocent is to admit the possibility of his guilt. Now they openly stood up for him.

And, although even the directors, most of whom had no acquaintance with the young man, were willing to suspend judgment until the period of his vacation had expired, there was a tension in the air all through the days that followed, and Truxton's firmest supporters were uneasy.

"If it had been anybody but Truxton!" Andy Stone would lament; "I say, Judson, if it were *you* we should know how to bear it!" And if Judson thought of no happy retort, he for once escaped any strictures upon his lack of humor. Andy Stone's sally was considered to be in questionable taste.

And, after all, the chief mourner on this occasion was Flynn. Somehow or other the old man had got wind of the trouble even before the bloodcurdling publication of it in the *Evening Spy*, and the genuineness of his sorrow was not to be questioned. The most marked indication of affliction was to be found in the fact that he had nothing to say on the subject. It was one morning, the latter part of the first week, that he had gone to

Rathbone for verification of the rumor which had reached him, and, upon Rathbone's admission that there was something they did not quite understand, he had retired definitively behind the *Morning Trumpeter*, from which retreat he only emerged upon compulsion. That he was preoccupied with other subjects of thought than the long words was evident from the fact that he was discovered more than once holding the newspaper upside-down.

The esteem and confidence which Flynn enjoyed among his colleagues was in nothing more clearly demonstrated than in the fact that it did not once occur to anyone to tax him with the indiscretion by means of which news of the trouble had found its way into the unscrupulous hands of the *Evening Spy*. Somebody had blundered, but no one thought of Flynn as the culprit.

The paragraph in the paper had given the finishing touch of tragedy to the situation, and although the bank authorities had succeeded in suppressing further mention of the affair in that or in other and more respectable sheets, the open stigma added not a little to the poignancy of the situation.

Truxton, meanwhile, was due on Monday morning, and, as the time drew near, all concerned—all but Flynn, that is to say—took heart of hope.

"I say, fellows," Harvey Winch remarked, towards noon on Saturday, "won't it be a 'sight for sair een' when Frank Truxton turns up here Monday morning!"

"I've been thinking he might happen in to-day," said Wilkinson, with a ponderous attempt at a light view of the case. "If he should be anywhere about he'd want his letters;" and the speaker mentally wished there had not been among the letters a communication from the Highflyer Mining and Milling Company of Cripple Creek, and that he had not been forced to admit as much to Mr. Smith. Truxton was straight enough, of course, but it was a pity for a young fellow to fool away his money on trash like that.

And even while the faithful Wilkinson was in the act of assuring himself that Truxton was "straight enough," the pilgrims were electrified by the sudden entrance of the missing clerk.

Truxton, as he entered the door, looked neither to the right nor to the left, but walked straight to the treasurer's private office; yet the mere sight of his lithe young figure, with the familiar carriage of the head, and the unfamiliar but firm and convincing lines of the deeply tanned countenance, revived their drooping spirits like a breath of fresh air in a suffocating enclosure.

"Thank the Lord, that's over!" was young Beardsley's pious exclamation.

Truxton found Mr. Smith alone at his desk. The vice-treasurer looked up as the young man entered, and he, too, felt the convincing force of his personality.

"Well, Truxton," he cried; "I'm glad to see you."

"Thank you, sir," and Truxton drew the fateful newpaper from his pocket. He had not once re-read the paragraph, but he knew every word of it.

"Perhaps you can tell me what this means," he said, laying the paper upon the desk, as if he could not bear to have it pass from his hand to another.

"Yes; we saw it. Most unfortunate, most unfortunate! Take a seat, won't you? We gave them a quietus, and we don't think it has been widely read."

Truxton declined the proffered chair.

"But what does it mean, sir?" he asked again.

"It means,"—and Mr. Smith contracted his brow, and scrutinized Truxton's face attentively,—"it means that when Plummer took over the cash on the eighth, he found it ten thousand dollars short!"

"Ten thousand dollars!" Truxton repeated. "Ten thousand dollars!"

As the young man stood pondering this statement, Henry Smith, who was a keen observer of his fellow-men, was aware of a marked change in him. The face was worn and tense, the figure seemed, somehow, more closely knit, more capable of resistance.

"Where were you when you saw this?" Smith asked.

"In the backwoods of Maine, camping on Mirror Pond."

"And that was?"

"Thursday afternoon."

"How did you get out so quickly?"

"I walked most of the night to Parlin Pond and got the stage for Skowhegan."

"H'm! I know the region. There's no night train from Skowhegan. How the deuce did you get here?"

"I got a fellow to drive me to Waterville and struck the five-fifty train this morning. We made connection with the eight-thirty-five train from Portland. We were nearly three minutes late here."

Truxton recited all this as carefully as if he had been in the witness-box, but all the time his brain was working, hammering away at one thing as it had been doing for the last forty-eight hours—namely, how could that gold certificate have got lost?

"Well, I'm glad to see you, Truxton, I'm glad to see you," the vice-treasurer reiterated; "and I rather guess that you and Plummer together can get at this thing."

"Mr. Smith," Truxton asked, suddenly, "do you know whether Plummer found that ten-thousand-dollar gold certificate all right?"

"Ten-thousand-dollar gold certificate? What the devil do you mean?"

"I gave Mr. Seymour ten thousand in bills for one certificate."

"Good Lord, Truxton! You must be off

your head! We never handle single certificates to that amount! There's never any occasion for it."

"I don't know anything about that," said Truxton; "but Mr. Seymour will remember it. Has he gone home for the day?"

An ugly suspicion crossed the vice-treasurer's mind.

"I suppose you did n't happen to know that Mr. Seymour sailed for Europe last week Tuesday?"

"Why, no! I don't know anything that has been going on for the last two weeks."

"It was generally known a week before you left town."

"Very likely." And the younger man's tone and bearing stiffened curiously.

Truxton had caught the shadow of mistrust on the vice-treasurer's face. It was worse than the public denunciation. But he did not flinch. He had had two days and nights in which to steel himself against any outward betrayal of feeling.

"There's nothing to prevent your verifying my statement," he remarked, quietly; "Mr. Seymour happened to mention to me that the transaction was made for the Seventh National."

Smith's face cleared.

"Of course, of course!" he said.

Smith's face cleared, but it never looked quite the same to Truxton again.

After a little more talk: "Do you know whether

my aunt, Miss Vickery, has been disturbed about this?" Truxton asked.

"I think not. We sent to inquire for your address on Tuesday, and on Wednesday, after the director's meeting, Mr. Caleb Ware went out to call upon her, and learn what he could. Mr. Ware, I think, has some family association with your aunt and he made a pretext of renewing an old acquaintance."

So Ruth's father had been to see Aunt Lucretia, —on her day, too, Truxton thought, with a melancholy ghost of sympathetic pleasure. He wondered whether Mr. Ware's face, as he talked with her of her nephew, had worn that intolerable expression that had played about the vice-treasurer's lips a moment ago. At least she would not have perceived it; her senses had not been sharpened in advance.

Suddenly Truxton took a seat rather abruptly.

"That's right," said Mr. Smith, his equanimity quite restored; "as soon as Plummer can be spared at the counter we'll have him up."

"It's very idiotic, sir," Truxton replied, in a tone of extreme self-disgust; "but—I believe I had better have some dinner before we do any more talking. I don't think I have eaten anything very lately, and I feel—hollow."

"You must be pretty well played out," Smith said, good-naturedly; "we shall look for you back soon after hours."

It had been only a passing seizure, and Truxton

walked straight enough as he left the office. A dozen friendly faces were turned towards him, but he did not look their way. Much less did he see a pair of sharp black eyes, watching him intently from the doorway of the back office. It was a busy day, and depositors were coming and going. As Truxton dodged one or two approaching figures, he suddenly came face to face with Flynn. The old man was standing just outside the doorway, on the upper step. He held his silk hat in his right hand, and his eyes blinked violently in the sun.

"Misther Trooxton," he exclaimed; "it's glad I am to see yez back!" and then, as Truxton shook hands with him, in rather a dazed and absent way, the old man drew close to him, and, while his voice dropped to a note of feeling it had never before betrayed, he said, "And Misther Trooxton, sorr, there's not a man in the bank that's not your frind, *whativer yez done wid the money!*"

Before Truxton could recover his equilibrium, after this astounding expression of sympathy, the queer old figure in shiny broadcloth had disappeared in the crowd. His mind loosed its hold on it almost as soon as it had vanished, and once more this young man who had annihilated space and tried to annihilate time to the attainment of a certain end, discovered that he was conscious of but one imperative need, namely, to stay the pangs of hunger at any cost.

And, since he had not observed those sharp black eyes in the rear doorway, he could not possibly be aware of the effect the sight of him had had upon their owner.

Tim, meanwhile, under cover of the shadowy recess, was masticating violently, in an effort to control emotions which suddenly threatened to take the upper hand of him. For be it known that this young apprentice in crime had made some little progress in the conquest over his own moral nature since that day, just two weeks ago, when he had sat disconsolate at the closed door of the bank.

On Sunday morning the yellow-journalism of the city had devoted itself to the special and particular glorification of a young bank messenger who, having absconded with a large sum of money, had been traced and brought back,—not ignominiously, but in a blaze of fame and splendor. Had he not been depicted as the central figure of a distinguished group of detectives and lawyers, lolling in elegant desuetude amid the velvety upholstery and gleaming mirrors of a Pullman car? Had not his name, accompanied by such flattering epithets as "daring," "reckless," "young in years but old in crime," been assigned a larger type than that accorded to the name of the President of the United States in connection with that high functionary's latest utterance upon a grave international complication? The glamour of the situation had fascinated Tim, and when Monday morning came he found it quite impossible to do anything so commonplace as to drop the money under the paying-teller's desk.

And so it came about that through those two weeks Tim had walked as in a dream of self-importance, feeling himself always on the point of taking the decisive step, of fleeing to Canada, pursued by vigilant detectives, and playing the leading part in whatever drama might spring from the exciting situation.

But Tim knew little of his own nature and of its hitherto dormant susceptibilities. When, on that bright September morning, Frank Truxton had entered the bank and walked straight to the treasurer's office ; when, from a distance, the lad had watched through the open door the grave faces of both men in earnest conversation ; above all, when Truxton had left the private office and walked away, with that desperate look on his face, not giving a glance to right or left, an overwhelming sense of personal affliction had seized upon Tim. He suddenly realized that it was an individual man, and not a soulless institution that he was injuring. He remembered, too, that no one in the bank had been so kind to him as Mr. Truxton. Had he not always had a pleasant word for Tim ? Had he not let him off with a bit of good-natured chaff when he, Tim, had carried about one of his letters without mailing it for a whole day and night ?—in the very pocket, Tim reflected, in which he had carried for a much longer period that enormous sum of money, the loss of which was to be a kind friend's ruin ! Above all, had he not given him a quarter for the circus, only three weeks ago, thanks to which munificence Tim had witnessed the most blood-curdling acrobatic feats and made acquaintance with the quips and cranks of a phenomenal clown ? And now they would doubtless send Mr. Truxton to jail and break his heart. It was almost broken already,—anybody could see that with half an eye !

At this juncture Tim pulled the chewing-gum from his mouth and stuffed it into his pocket. In some vague way he felt that he was doing penance by this momentary renunciation of his dearest solace. It was not fitting that he should chew gum while his victim suffered.

As he stood in the shadow, casting about him, dejectedly, for some means of restoring the money without incriminating himself, his eye fell upon the old linen coat which he had fetched for Mr. Truxton on that memorable Saturday. He remembered the " Thank you, Tim! " he had got for the small service. There was not another man in the bank who would have found it worth while to say " thank you." Tim sidled up to the coat, as it hung there, and laid his face against it, and slowly a big tear squeezed its way out of each of those sharp black eyes, and was viciously rubbed off—not without carrying some foreign deposit with it. And then,—Tim had an inspiration !

Glancing furtively about, to assure himself that he was not observed, he thrust his hand into his trousers pocket and pulled out the much crumpled gold certificate which he had so often fingered and gloated over. With another quick look to right and left, such as a squirrel will give before making deposit of a nut in a hollow tree, he jammed the much-adventured bill into an outside pocket of the linen coat.

"Tim!"

The sudden sound of his name sent an earthquake shock through his system! It was only Old Barry, who had dropped the cap of his stylographic pen and wanted Tim to find it. And, while the boy pounced with alacrity upon the missing pen-cap, and a deaf woman at the counter, being asked her name, persisted in replying, with bland patience, "Forty, yes; forty dollars!" the old coat hung, limp and neglected, in the dark corner, and evinced no intention of divulging the secret that had been entrusted to it.

But Tim, in his queer, twisted little soul, believed that he had made restitution; and so cheered was he by the removal of the oppressive incubus he had so long carried about with him, that he hastily repaired, after bank hours, to a certain floating pier at the foot of a flight of slimy green steps, where he relieved his feelings by practising a double-shuffle learned of the clown at the circus. But, alas! as his spirits rose he became reckless, and, forgetting the manifest insecurity of the little stage on which he was executing this difficult feat, he lost his balance and came down with a broken arm and sprained ankle on the treacherous pier.

It was a limp little figure that the hospital people carried up the narrow, slippery steps an hour later, and the small, haggard face was drawn with anguish. The hospital people, marvelling at his pluck and endurance, never guessed that the little Mick was upheld by the consciousness that no certificate for ten thousand dollars lurked in his trousers pocket!

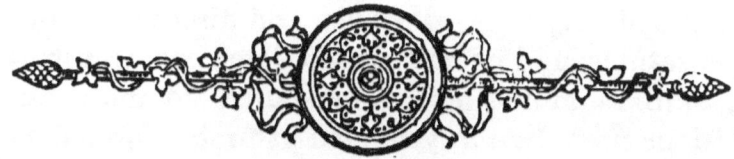

CHAPTER XVIII.

POOR EVERYBODY!

IT is perhaps given to few persons to take things as easily as Frank Truxton had done up to this time. Those three qualities which Harkness Dole had commented upon, namely: good sense, good perceptions, and good humor, had proved a sufficient equipment for such crises of life as he had heretofore encountered. By force of one or the other of them he had found himself easily equal to each situation which had presented itself; by virtue of all three he had, from the outset, made light of sacrifices and discovered compensations, and he had even of late been acquiring a skill in moulding circumstances to more ambitious uses than any he had at first imagined.

Now, of a sudden, he was brought face to face with a situation demanding something different from those " domestic virtues " of which he had spoken so disparagingly. Here was a dilemma which involved, first of all, acute mental suffering. Somehow or other he had got to brace himself to meet that, while, at the same time, he seemed denied the relief of active conflict.

On Saturday evening, after a fruitless interview with Plummer and the vice-treasurer, he had at least had the resource of collecting rents and somewhat straightening out the fortnight's accounts, and that night he had slept the sleep of utter exhaustion. When he awoke, his soul revolted against the day. Perceiving which, he at once took himself in hand and became, in very self-defence, the hardest possible master to himself.

As a first step in that bracing process which was so manifestly necessary, he decreed that he was to go to church with Miss Vickery—to face the little local congregation among whom he was well aware that the *Evening Spy* was widely read. As he walked up the main aisle to the family pew, he thought it highly probable that the tall old woman at his side was the only wholly unconscious person present, and he was amazed to find how little he minded this presumable curiosity and suspicion in the abstract, when compared with that one shadow of mistrust that had crossed the vice-treasurer's face.

From the Reverend Mr. Dillaway he learned, on this occasion, that life is a discipline—a general proposition which he was obliged to accept, though he found himself curiously antagonized by the preacher's manner of establishing it. Nevertheless, he listened respectfully to his aunt's encomiums upon this admirer of her favorite poet, and he cheerfully assured her that he did not see how anyone could be better fitted for the post he occupied than the reverend gentleman in question.

As a further step in the process of bracing, Truxton brought himself to tell his aunt, at their noonday meal, something of the life in camp, though the exercise was about as agreeable as one and another method of slow torture, the instruments of which he had studied in certain mediæval chambers of horror.

In the afternoon he allowed himself a long tramp into the country. He might run away all he liked, he told himself, there was not much that he could escape from. But at least he could get out of the city, this horrible, hard, uncompromising conglomeration of bricks and paving-stones, of men and women who read the papers and make complacent note of the fact that a man's name has been dragged in the mud and rendered unfit to pass the lips of decent people. His name! His name! It was the thought of his name that kept dull, monotonous time to the tramp of his feet upon the pavement. The truth had never before been brought home to him, that a man's name stood for the vital part of him; that to sully his name was to sully his very soul. Somehow the rest of it did not seem so important. And here the pavement ended, and the sound of his own feet became less insistent on the gravel walk.

Of course this disaster meant financial ruin. The money was gone; that was clear. He should make good the loss to the bank, but it would be at the sacrifice not only of the little he possessed, but of whatever he had hoped for. Nor was that all. He should lose his place, his means of livelihood; the bank examiners would see to that, even though, by a miracle, the personal bias of the authorities might counsel leniency.

Furthermore,—and he experienced a grim satisfaction in enumerating all the different heads under which his misfortunes ranged themselves,—furthermore, he would be hopelessly debarred from any other position of trust. And here he was again at the starting-point—his name. His personal friends might be as loyal as they would, and he could not, even in his most despairing moment conceive of his actual character being impugned by those who knew him; his good name,—that was lost, and in comparison with that the rest mattered not a whit.

Presently, a mile beyond the city limits, he came opposite a little knoll crowned with pine-trees, and involuntarily his feet took that direction. He threw himself down like the veriest tramp on the pine-needles, and buried his face in them, and for the moment his spirit was appeased.

All this time he had been holding the very thought of Ruth at arm's length; now it drew near in the deep, strong aroma of the earth and the pines, and there was healing in it. For the first time in three days he allowed himself to dwell upon the memory of her face as she had stood beside him, upon the tone and gesture with which she had said : " They are as fit for me as for you !" Yes, there was a spirit of loyalty in Ruth that would make her a thousand times more ready to share a man's adversity than his prosperity. To share it ? Had it come to that ?

A sudden, exultant certainty possessed him and he sprang to his feet to meet it. He looked across a squalid little group of houses below there, to a line of hills beyond. An autumn haze rested upon them and transformed them; they were the eternal hills, ethereal, brooding, fraught with infinite suggestion; they were like Ruth's face—a thought of God !

He lingered on the little eminence whence the hills were visible ; he lingered upon the thought of Ruth. And from the thought of Ruth he slowly and surely gathered strength to renounce her.

There was nothing dramatic about this resolve of Truxton's; he himself scarcely realized its force and reach. It was only a quiet, profound setting of his nature against any advantage to be gained through that compassionateness, that chivalry in Ruth—there was no better word for it than that— which he had the insight to recognize as the keynote of her character.

There is rarely anything inspiriting in renunciation ; and when, an hour later, in the gathering dusk, he walked up the well-worn path between the lilac-bushes, dusty now, and parched, after the summer heats, life seemed to him to have sunk to an eternal level. He looked up at the old house, and all his pride in it was gone. He saw only its dinginess and its decay. Aunt Lucreatia would die, presently, the place would be sold and degraded to the character of its surroundings; and he? He should live on, like the perennial lilac-bushes, marking a path that led, not to a home any longer, only to mean and sordid things.

On the hall table he found a card with a few words written in a small, incisive hand, across the face of it. Harkness Dole had called. But how could that be? He was in his own quarters at the Singleton Chambers. Would Truxton come and have a picnic-supper with him at half-past seven?

But Dole had said nothing about coming up to town. What could it mean? Had there been an accident? Had anybody got hurt? Had Ruth—? How absurd he was! Just because he, Frank Truxton, had come to grief, he need not interpret every chance incident in terms of tragedy. He might certainly have the satisfaction of seeing Harkness Dole. Dole always had something to talk about; he was always worth while.

"I had no idea you were coming up," he said, as Dole bade him welcome.

"Nor I," said Dole. "But here I am. It is n't half bad in the city to-day."

"No?" Truxton demurred. "It seemed to me—twice that!"

The room in which the table was laid was in reality a sort of bachelor's den, though there were certain conveniences for serving a casual meal like the present, and the serving-man had the air of belonging to the establishment. The main furnishing of the apartment consisted of books, the shelves reaching nearly to the ceiling and giving to the place a sombre character not inappropriate to the somewhat ascetic personality of the master.

As they took their seats at table, it struck the guest as rather singular that he should not shrink just now from facing this severe, sarcastic countenance. Somehow he felt more sure of comprehension at Dole's hands than at those of the men with whom he had long been on terms of easy good-comradeship.

"I brought you no end of messages," Dole was saying; "I hope you won't expect me to get them all straight."

"Well, no; that would be too much. But what did—Dan say, for instance?"

"He said, 'Tell him when he gets tired of being in a hurry he had better come back!'"

Truxton laughed.

"Dan rather resented being hauled along so fast after we left the canoe."

"But he's your friend, Truxton! He'll never forget that snake!"

"Jolly old boy, that snake was, to get in the way of my gun! I'm only glad you did n't have to pay the piper, Dole!"

Dole was carving a chicken.

"I thought you might be tired of game," he remarked, as he severed a joint, with one persuasive incision, "so I did n't order partridges—or muskrat!"

"I hope, at least, you are going to top off with flapjacks!" Truxton retorted. He flattered himself that he was doing very well, that he was handling a difficult situation in rather a debonair manner; and Dole was very much of the same opinion.

Nor did the latter see cause to modify his view when, half an hour later, they were left to themselves, and openly broached the subject of Truxton's embarrassment. It may be, indeed, that Dole's blazing wood-fire, seconded by a *Margarita Extra*, did its part toward taking the edge off the situation.

Truxton was ready to tell all he knew about the disaster, and little enough it was. A gold certificate had somehow got itself out of the cash-box, out of the safe, apparently out of the universe, in the interval between Truxton's closing the box and Plummer's opening it.

"So, you know the very piece of money that is gone! Won't that make it easier to find?"

"I don't see how. At any rate, it eliminates all possibility of any error in the books. If it were not for that we should feel sure that it had been some incredible slip there. Figures are such inveterate liars!"

"Do bank figures lie? That is contrary to the popular impression."

"Oh, yes; they lie fast enough, only they are pretty sure to get found out, sooner or later."

Dole was leaning back in his leathern armchair, gazing through the small rings of smoke that curled out of his cigarette.

"How about this other chap that came after you? Plummer is his name?"

The insinuation was very slight, but Truxton bridled instantly.

"What! Plummer?" he exclaimed. "Why, Plummer is as straight as I am—and twice as careful."

"That's all very well," said Dole; "but he's human, I suppose. Now you know positively that you put the thing into the box, and, as he was not looking for it, he can't know as positively whether he took it out. At any rate it seems to me it lies between you two."

"That is because you don't know Plummer," Truxton insisted, with stubborn, boyish loyalty.

Dole looked at him half quizzically for a moment, and then the face of the elder man softened, as it rarely did.

"I at least have the advantage of *your* acquaintance, Truxton," he said; "and I don't mind your knowing that I prize it highly!"

For the first time, Truxton changed countenance; a wave of feeling broke up, for an instant, the tension which had been apparent under his light talk and indifferent manner.

"Thanks," he said; "that's worth hearing!"

"I am glad it does not offend you," Dole remarked, with a return to his habitual manner; "because I came up to town on purpose to tell you that, and—to ask of you a favor. It's always well to preface a petition with a compliment, is it not?"

"I believe so," Truxton returned, with a short laugh; "and I'm glad to hear that you have a favor to ask. There is scarcely anything I should not be in a position to do for you, Dole!" The bitter tang of this little speech was pathetically out of character. Dole ignored it, although it had not been lost upon him.

"First, tell me what you propose to do," he demanded.

"What I propose to do? I thought it was you that——"

"What do you propose to do?" Dole persisted. "I suppose you'll hardly wait for the bank to take the initiative?"

"Hardly!"

"And you?"

"I? I shall pay up."

"You are able to, then?"

"Yes."

"You have n't got a ten-thousand-dollar balance, I take it, uninvested?"

"No; I shall realize."

"Not in a hurry, I hope."

"Well, the thing strikes me as rather urgent!"

Dole leaned forward, with slow deliberation, and turned one of the logs, causing the fire to blaze up in good shape.

"Look here, Truxton," he said, as his tongs closed upon a piece of glowing wood which he carefully placed on top of the pile, "could n't we bridge this thing over, between us? That real-estate of yours requires time."

"Between us?" Truxton repeated; "how—between us?"

"Well—the fact is, I 've got some bonds that are just about to expire, and——"

"They are not going to expire *between us!*" Frank replied, rather grimly.

Dole tossed the stump of his cigarette into the fire before he said, with a persuasiveness which was seldom exercised and rarely resisted: "I want you to use this money—at least until I think of something better to do with it."

But Truxton closed his ears and hardened his heart.

"Sorry to disoblige you, Dole," he said, roughly; "but this is a case where I have got to —paddle my own canoe!"

"A single paddle is n't safe in rough weather," was Dole's prompt rejoinder.

"Then I shall have to swim for it."

There was a pause before either spoke again. Then the elder of the two observed, musingly, "It 's bad to capsize on the open sea."

"Perhaps so,—though I take it it 's not the drowning that hurts."

Dole sprang to his feet, with an impatient gesture, and Truxton, too, stood up. The host reached down a couple of pipes from a rack over the chimney-piece.

"Cigarettes are pesky artificial things," he said; "let 's try a pipe and talk sense. To begin with, put yourself in my place."

"That 's easily done," Truxton assented. "The thing that can't be done is for you to put yourself in my place."

Dole shrugged his shoulders, impatiently, as he stuffed the tobacco well down into his pipe. Then, resuming his seat, and leaning back in his chair, he looked across at Truxton and, half closing his eyes, he asked: "Would you mind telling me your idea of a friend, and what he 's for?"

And Truxton flung his head back as he used to do when they were in the heat of discussion out there in the cool silences of the forest, and he said, with a ring of feeling in his voice: "*You* are my idea of a friend, Dole!"

Dole bowed his head with mock ceremony.

"And just what is his use?" he queried.

"Mainly, I think, to keep the life in a man! See here, Dole! There's nothing I know how to say about your coming up, and all that,—only you never do need to have things explained. But —when a man has only got one thing left, he hangs on to it. And I think you'll have to let me hang on to what I've got."

Dole was too good an antagonist not to know when he was beaten.

"Very well," he said; "I'm sorry I've been bothersome. And will this straighten things out for you at the bank?"

"Why, yes; they don't want to prosecute. All they want is their money."

"And there'll be no interruption in your——"

"Oh, I can't go back, of course!" Truxton spoke with quiet self-control; this was what he had been drilling himself in for three days past. And Dole, glancing at the face turned toward the firelight, saw in it the same resolution which governed the voice.

"I suppose there is no one who doubts you?" and he felt quite safe in hazarding the suggestion.

"No; I think not,—now. But a bank is a peculiar concern. These things have to be somewhat cut-and-dried. Besides, there are the bank examiners. No," he added, with another short laugh, "I don't think I am likely to adorn another position of trust!"

"And what is your plan?"

"To forage for something else.—That's an interesting pair of faces over there," and he glanced toward the mantelpiece.

"Yes," said Dole, accepting the change of subject, and, rising, he handed Truxton a frame of stamped leather, containing two cabinet photographs. The one represented a thin-visaged man of fifty or thereabouts, dressed in the fashion of twenty years ago. The face, which resembled Dole's, was handsomer than his, but not as good.

"My father and my stepmother," the host remarked, seating himself once more, and relighting his pipe.

The stepmother, Truxton remembered, was Ruth's aunt. He thought it the saddest-looking countenance he had ever seen—all the sadder for the effort at a smile which curved the lips but did not light the eyes.

"It is a noble face," he said.

"Yes," Dole answered, quietly assuming that Truxton did not refer to his father. "She is said to have been very like Ruth in her youth. I can just remember her at the time of the marriage. It was twenty years later that she died."

Truxton experienced a strange sensation; it was almost as if a direct connection had been hinted at between the two events.

"I can see the resemblance," he said; and, rising, he replaced the frame upon the shelf. He had a curious feeling of having opened the wrong door.

"Yes; they are alike," Dole repeated, thoughtfully; "and my father and I are alike. Something singular about family resemblances," he added, with a sudden drop into generalization.

They did more smoking than talking for the rest of the visit, and their talk was of indifferent matters.

As Truxton rose to take his leave Dole remarked: "There are all those messages that I have n't given. I think there was only one person in camp who did not send you one."

"Caleb, I suppose."

"No; Ruth!" It was the first time Ruth's name had been mentioned, in the present tense, so to speak. "I asked her if she had a message for you, and she said, no, she should hope to see you soon. Her exact words were,"—and he passed his hand absently across the edge of the stamped leather frame,—"her exact words were: 'There is nothing you could say to him from me that he does not know already.' It was quite what I should expect," he added, judicially; "Ruth never mixes things!"

"Miss Ware was very kind the other day," Truxton said, quite steadily. "She understood at once." His hand was on the door-handle. As he turned to go, he said: "Will you tell her that I was grateful, although I did not seem so?"

"Considering her views on the subject of messages," Dole observed, "I should say you had better wait and tell her yourself!"

The door was open now.

"I'm afraid I should have to wait so long that she—might have forgotten all about it!" upon which the speaker stepped across the threshold, and, with a hasty "Good-bye," pulled the door to.

Dole made no motion to detain him. He only paused a moment where he stood, facing the closed door, and, presently, he turned on his heel and sauntered back into the room. The air was heavy with tobacco smoke. He stepped to a window and flung the sash open; then, returning to the fireplace, he rested his arm upon the chimney-shelf, and stood looking down into the glowing ashes.

"Poor Truxton!" he said to himself.

There was one of those absorbing little incidents going on among the sticks which only a wood-fire knows how to improvise. He bent his head still lower, apparently quite intent upon the little drama enacting on the hearth. Presently his lips moved, and "Poor Ruth!" he murmured, quite audibly.

Upon which, as if recalled to himself by the sound of his own voice, he lifted his head and found himself face to face with those pictured countenances in which lurked, half hidden, half revealed, the tragedy of his life, which he had decreed should close the tragedy of his race. For the first time in many years he permitted himself to fold the frame together and lay it away from his sight. As he did so, his severe, well disciplined features betrayed no emotion; there was only a look, half wistful, half satirical, about his thin, clean-cut lips as he murmured: " Poor everybody!"

CHAPTER XIX.

FLYNN'S ROMANCE BY ADOPTION.

HAPPILY for Flynn's "protejay," the number of his friends was not limited to those who possessed sensibilities as keen and perceptions as delicate as his own. If Harkness Dole found himself baffled by a feeling in Truxton which he himself understood and respected, if Will Shepleigh, when he arrived a day or two later, was met and vanquished by the same difficulty in his ardent attempt to set things straight, it was no more than might well have been anticipated. Assailed by an intolerable misfortune, touched by the breath of ill-fame, the boy's whole nature had stiffened and hardened in stubborn resistance.

It was much like the involuntary knitting of the muscles against a fall, to which ill-advised procedure so many a broken bone is due. Your trained huntsman can "come a cropper" uninjured, simply because he has learned not to brace himself against it. But Frank Truxton had had no experience in the sort of tumble which means disgrace and ruin, and he knew no better, poor fellow, than to break his bones, or, rather, to break his heart, against his own mistaken heroism.

Not only did he reject the proffered aid of Dole and Shepleigh; he resolutely thrust from him a far more precious friendliness. For on Tuesday there came a note from Ruth, asking him to come and see her at her own house. She was going on into the country the following day, but she was to be in town that afternoon and evening, and she should count upon seeing him.

Truxton wrote his answer almost without reflection: and indeed where was the need of reflection, now, when his course of action must be governed by an unalterable resolve? Neither did he hesitate as to the form his refusal should take. He wrote his precise reason, because he felt that nothing short of perfect sincerity could ever serve between him and Ruth.

He said :

"MY DEAR MISS WARE:

"I can not come to see you while things are as they are. It would not be right, and that is all I have left to go by. By holding on to that I am going to pull through, and one of these days,"—

(the little phrase was inexpressibly consoling to him)—

"one of these days, when we are old folks, I shall come and tell you that I was not ungrateful.

"Yours faithfully,
"FRANK TRUXTON."

The note was written in perfect good faith, and Truxton honestly believed it to be final. He was even couscious of a sense of relief, such as a man may experience who has actually undergone the dreaded amputation of a leg or an arm—a sense of having now but to adjust his life to changed conditions. The changed conditions might prove to be well-nigh intolerable, but that was another matter. Meanwhile the process of adjustment went on.

On Tuesday morning there had been a meeting of the bank directors—the Pilgrim Fathers, as they were irreverently called—at which solemn function Truxton had been invited to appear. The occasion had been singularly lacking in dramatic point. The defaulting clerk had merely told what he knew as to the disaster, and stated his willingness and ability eventually to reimburse the bank ; in consideration of which extenuating circumstance it was voted to accept the young man's resignation. So that, after all, Truxton was technically correct when he told his aunt that he had himself severed his connection with the bank, and that he proposed devoting his attention, for a time, at least, to his tenement-house interests. And, indeed, these proved sufficiently absorbing for the moment.

The sale of his own property was entrusted to the firm through whom he had purchased it, and on whom were not lost the improvements which had been accomplished in the interval. The head of the firm, one of the strong real-estate men of the city, had a long talk with Truxton, in the course of which he warmly endorsed the young man's methods from a business standpoint. He even went so far as to hint at a possible co-operation between them, which might prove profitable to both. For Truxton had told him of his projected lease of the estate adjoining his own, and of his intention of developing a business on these lines, which gave him something of the status of a colleague with the more regular real-estate concerns.

The lease in question had been drawn up during his absence from town, and was now duly executed; and from this undertaking, together with the commissions on the Hitchcock property, he hoped to realize a sufficient income to keep the wolf from the door. He had a plan for appropriating as an office a certain dark little den on the first floor of the big block which he was leasing. It was a dreary hole, but rather an advantageous foothold from which to handle just that sort of business.

Truxton had not taken this lease without giving his man a chance to withdraw. The other party to the transaction, as the Honorable Bowdoin J. Wheeler would doubtless have styled himself, was an elderly lawyer of the kind usually designated as "conservative but safe." No; he had no intention of withdrawing from his agreement; yes, he had understood that Mr. Truxton was leaving the bank under somewhat embarrassing circumstances. He had informed himself on that head. One of the directors, Mr. Caleb Ware, had assured him that Mr. Truxton's behavior was considered entirely creditable; in fact, Mr. Ware had gone so far as to express himself as willing to vouch personally for Mr. Truxton's integrity, had there been any necessity for his so doing.

And if this simple statement of fact sent a disconcerting tide of emotion to Truxton's heart he kept his head so completely that the interview merely confirmed the Honorable Wheeler's good opinion of him as a young man who neither wasted words nor neglected details. In fact, as afterwards transpired, it struck the old gentleman that a man with a good deal of trust property on his hands might make him useful in behalf of his clients. There was his old friend Holcomb's widow, for instance. He had thought of advising a change in her investments; but perhaps she could not do better than to retain that block of houses at the City End, if this young man would consent to handle it.

But, as if this process of gradual rehabilitation had been too slow to suit the purposes of a fate which could not long tolerate the incongruity of Frank Truxton as the central figure of a tragic situation, a quicker solution of the difficulty was in process than any which could have been anticipated. And this solution was to occur at the hands, not of a Harkness Dole, nor of a Will

Shepleigh, who, as we have seen, were handicapped by a sympathetic understanding of just such obstacles as the nature of their would-be beneficiary presented, but of one who, knowing them not, was incapable of finding them a stumbling-block.

In a neat tenement at the top of that block which was in imminent danger of passing into other and less liberal hands, the face of Katie and the blue-glass vase were an hourly admonition, if such had been needed, to the one friend of Truxton's who was quite unhampered by too delicate sensibilities.

Barney Flynn had his own views upon the bank disaster, and these were so simple and to the point that he found no difficulty in acting in accordance with them. The best friend he had in the world was in trouble; it was not for Flynn to say how he got there. Perhaps he lost the money; perhaps he " borried it " first and lost it afterward. Flynn had not been in the employ of the Pilgrim Savings Bank for forty years without becoming aware that it was a very usual thing for even the rich and the great, for millionaires and corporations to borrow of it, to divert a portion of its fabulous resources to their own use. As to the more essential features of the transaction, he had never taken pains to inform himself; and, if he could not avoid the inference that a loan of this character was usually made with the knowledge and consent of the bank authorities, that was a detail which he scorned to take into consideration. If "Misther Trooxton" had borrowed a sum of money—if he had done so, mind you— he had doubtless had good and sufficient reasons for so doing. And Flynn, sitting beneath the portrait of Katie, allowed his imagination to be visited by another young and charming personality.

The old man, in his lonely eyrie, had found the keenest gratification in weaving a romance about this young fellow who, of all the world, had succeeded in drawing near to the modest little shrine of Flynn's own romance without once offending or affrighting its keeper. Without laying aside, for a moment, his armor of assumed indifference to things of sentiment, Flynn had secretly felt his heart warm to the covert sympathy of one whose perceptions were too delicate to confess themselves. Flynn would have died sooner than admit that he had carried Truxton's occasional floral offerings home to Katie. Yet, jealously as he guarded his own spiritual sanctities, there was scarcely a sacrifice of material things that he would not have made for the sake of furthering his "protejay's" interests in an affair of a like nature.

If "Misther Trooxton" wanted the girl "wid the nate figger on her," and who was so commendably "spry on her feet,"—why, he must have her! That was the whole matter in a nutshell. And if the bank was going to be hard on him it was for him, Barney Flynn, to see that the boy did not suffer.

From the first rumor of trouble, Flynn had been inclined to regard this as his opportunity. If he had fallen upon an unnatural silence, if he had taken to reading the *Morning Trumpeter* upside down, it was because he was preoccupied with a plan by means of which he was intending to save the situation. And when, on Truxton's return, one glance at the young man's face had convinced him that the case was serious, his own course had become clear.

It was perhaps fortunate that Flynn's good-will and self-devotion were not a mere matter of sentiment, for that would scarcely have got itself satisfactorily expressed. The one attempt at verbal consolation which he had made was not so happily chosen as to augur well for its efficacy in the long run. That sinister phrase, "whativer yez done wid the money," might have rankled in the mind of anybody but Truxton. To him, to be sure, it was peculiarly, grotesquely acceptable, and for the simple reason that his sense of humor found refreshment in it. Everybody else was changed; his whole easy-going, amusing world of impressions was keyed to unnatural seriousness. Almost every man he knew was oppressively considerate, abnormally kind. But would anybody ever again take a liberty with him? Would anybody ever again make light of him? Flynn, at least, was unchanged; Flynn's views, at least, would never be slavishly adapted to the conventional standard. Flynn was his friend, " whativer he done wid the money !"

Yet at how great a cost to himself Flynn was prepared to act the part of friend, no one could have foretold, for no one guessed the extent of his pecuniary resources. That the old man had led a frugal life, that he had accumulated a full book at the Pilgrim almost before the memory of man, was well known. The interest on his sixteen hundred dollars was drawn semi-annually, and it was understood that at least two other savings institutions were enriched with the overflow, together with such further sums as continued to detach themselves from his monthly wages. In fact, it was well understood that Flynn was a capitalist, and if his colleagues occasionally indulged in strictures upon his pet extravagances—in the matter of " pin-scarfs," for instance—they never felt any real anxiety as to his solvency in the future.

Yet not one of the pilgrims was aware of the full extent of his wealth, nor that its acquisition dated from that melancholy event of which Flynn had spoken to Truxton, the previous winter, with such callous indifference. Indeed, if the truth were known, the old man's attitude at the time of his brother's death—that brother at whose bedside he had been present when he was " haivin' his last puff ! "—had been due to a distorted sense of propriety in view of the fact that Patrick had made Barney his sole heir.

Patrick Flynn had been an ill-natured old curmudgeon of the money-getting variety. He had survived three wives, apparently in deliberate pursuance of his openly expressed resolve to leave no widow, and the untimely demise of several children had left him unembarrassed by the consideration of prospective orphans. He had not been on speaking terms with any of his relatives except Barney, who had taken him and his idiosyncrasies in the philosophic spirit of indulgence usual with the pilgrim sage.

A decorous affliction might have been anticipated in Flynn, had it not been for the shock of finding himself the heir. Under the embarrassment of being thus singled out for enrichment, however, he had deemed it proper to adopt a tone of easy indifference, perhaps with an ill-defined notion of proving that his tears, or what stands for tears in an elderly, self-contained mourner, were not to be bought!

Be that as it may, when Flynn determined to mend the fortunes of his best friend, it was with the inspiring assurance, conceded to so few of us, that his resources were equal to his good intentions.

Nor was his determination to devote the bulk of a handsome fortune to the uses of another quite as striking an exercise of heroism as would appear. Regrettable as the necessity is, of detracting from the merit of a good deed, it is only proper, in the cause of accuracy, to admit that

Flynn had no inordinate estimate of the value of money. If he led a frugal life, it was neither because he thought it his duty to save money, nor, far less, because of any miserly inclination to hoard. He had been in the habit of spending what he wished; but his desires had been limited. When he had purchased a gilt frame for Katie's picture, he had done so regardless of expense; when he had elected to wear a silk hat as being the covering best beseeming his years and dignity, he had been well aware that decorum was to be maintained only at the price of a frequent and considerable financial outlay. If he preferred a clay pipe, he at least used the best tobacco. But, when all was told, his requirements had been very small, and he had simply placed in the savings-bank a legitimate surplus.

Nor was the approach of old age a consideration to which Flynn gave much thought. He cherished a comfortable assurance that he should hardly outlive his capacity for wetting " spinges " and fetching ledgers, and his views upon mortuary expenses were very modest. Once, indeed, when he was convicted of having contributed an unconscionable sum toward the burial of a brother-in-law's mother, he had openly admitted that he could have " buried himsilf for half the money!"

Hence it will be seen that, in realizing upon a parcel of bonds which had been reposing under his bed for months, in the bottom of a box labelled " SOAP," and in drawing out all the money he possessed in savings-banks other than the Pilgrim, he was not performing an act of superhuman heroism. Furthermore, from the moment that he learned that a single bill, large though it was, represented Truxton's loss, his line of action had been materially simplified.

And so it came about that one afternoon, two or three weeks after Truxton's return from camp, and the discovery of the exact nature of his loss, the transaction was complete, and Flynn found himself in possession of a crisp new certificate for ten thousand dollars, which he had purchased at the Sub-Treasury. It was too late in the day for him to gain admission to the bank, and to do so, as shall presently transpire, was essential to the execution of his little scheme.

When Flynn went to bed that night, he did a very peculiar thing. And, as a preliminary, he took out the valuable bit of paper which he had come into possession of, and examined it long and carefully, wondering, the while, at the unpretentiousness of its superficial aspect. This, in itself, was not an improbable procedure on his part, nor was it strange, all things considered, that he elected to do so in face of the picture of Katie. He might well have fancied that those kindly, sentimental eyes regarded him the more affectionately, the more approvingly, for the offering he was about to make on the altar of his little romance by adoption.

But when the time came for seeking a place of

safety for the money, his mind did not once recur to the soap-box, nor did he for a moment entertain the very obvious expedient of hiding it under his pillow. Ignoring all such commonplace devices, he stepped across the room to the old carpet-covered sofa, and, kneeling upon it, he lifted from the bracket the blue glass vase in which a sprig of mignonette was blooming, and set it carefully upon the neatly folded certificate. After which little ceremony, he turned away, and, picking up the lamp, passed into the adjoining room, where soon the old man was sleeping the deep sleep of a trustful child.

CHAPTER XX.

HUMBLE HOSPITALITIES.

TO Truxton's mind it had long been clear that work and work only was the means to most ends, but it was only in the days following his enforced retirement from the Pilgrim Savings Bank that he learned its intrinsic value as a mental and moral stimulus.

He had begun the week in a condition of mind which might almost be called passive; if he had braced himself, it had been not so much to action as to endurance. Happily, the necessity for action presenting itself at the very outset rendered endurance less difficult, and by the time Saturday night came he was almost too tired and too preoccupied to know that he was miserable.

Business had accumulated rapidly on his hands as the week went on. Not only had there been the directors' meeting, the interviews with Wheeler, and various consultations and explanations looking to the sale of his own block, but innumerable small, practical details had crowded in upon him. Repairs were to be pushed, workpeople to be prodded, tenants to be conciliated or otherwise dealt with. He hardly knew whether he was more desirous of making a success of his new venture, or of handing over the old in good shape to whatever purchaser might be obliging enough to present himself. He had also set his heart upon having a full rent-roll for the delectation of Mrs. Hitchcock upon her return to town in November.

All this detail he labored over with a zest of which he did not himself quite approve. After he had gained some small end for which he had wrestled well, such a sense of satisfaction took possession of him that he was quite abashed when he became conscious of it. At another moment, under the exhilaration of a difficulty conquered, he would become singularly sceptical as to certain painful facts which he had considered established beyond peradventure. His name, for instance; was it really in such a bad way? Just what was the blemish on it? Did anybody imagine that——?

Then, with a rush of shame, he would remember that there was plenty of room for such imaginings, that, at least, anybody might!—that, indeed, Mr. Smith *had*,—if only for a moment. That when a man's name was open to doubt, the less said about it, the less thought about it, the better; and he would throw himself upon his weekly accounts with exclusive attention; or he would adopt energetic measures for the eviction of one of that class of tenants in whom a notice to quit arouses an insane desire to remain, and who, by some mysterious provision of nature, are able to put forth a thousand small, clinging tentacles to meet the one emergency with which they seem fitted to cope withal.

Yet, on the whole, between the unchastened risings of a sanguine temperament and the severe repressions of a youthful intolerance of compromise, Truxton managed to keep himself pretty well in hand, and when, on the morning of the third Wednesday, the mail brought him an unlooked-for temptation, he was able to resist it with a fair degree of composure.

The temptation came in the form of a note from young Caleb Ware, already returned to college, asking him to go with him into the country for the following Sunday.

"It will seem pretty slow at our house, after camping out,"

Caleb wrote;

"but the leaves are bully this year."

Truxton flung off a hasty line of refusal and got it sealed and stamped and posted in a heat of self-immolation which left him breathless. After which he suffered a severe collapse.

There was no further use in any sophistries touching the true state of things. If his name had been clear he should have gone to see that "bully" foliage. There must be something radically wrong about a man's name if it did not permit of his doing a little thing like that!

By way of consolation he called upon Mattie Tripe that afternoon, ostensibly to inquire whether the cord in the kitchen window had been repaired. He had not seen Mattie when he called for the rent the previous week; he was always sorry to miss her.

He found the little woman patiently inserting a patch into Jimmy's best jacket, humming softly to herself the while. Things must be going right with them. She jumped to her feet and placed a chair for him, wiping off the seat with the skirt of her dress, in imitation of her grown-up neighbors; and then, with the instinctive hospitality which is characteristic of the very poor, she brought him a plate, a knife, and an apple.

Truxton had learned never to decline such courtesies. Indeed, he was himself convinced that he owed one of his best tenants to the fortitude with which he had joined the family at supper and partaken largely of corned-beef and cabbage —a form of sustenance which he particularly detested. Nor had his gastronomic experiments been limited to such home-brew as this. Passover wine and unleavened bread were well known to his unappreciative palate, while certain nameless concoctions, highly seasoned, but nondescript, and emanating from a large black kettle, had formed a bond of union between himself and more than one family of handsome, warm-hearted Italians.

As little Mattie approached him, bearing the harmless form of nourishment with which she had elected to regale him, she lifted her solemn eyes to his, and remarked that Miss Ware had sent them a whole barrelful of apples yesterday.

"That must have been a pleasant surprise," Truxton observed, with hypocritical casualness, as he accepted the little offering.

"No," the matter-of-fact Mattie replied; "it wa'n't no s'prise. Miss Ware, she 'd promised to send 'em, 'n' so she 'd sent 'em!"

As Truxton tasted the noble fruit, it struck him that he had never before appreciated its quality, and his mind reverted, with a curious relenting, to that moment of weakness in our common ancestor which is supposed to have been fraught with such disastrous consequences to us all. Doubtless, he thought to himself, if Adam had refused the apple, that gold certificate would never have got lost; yet, what an excellent fruit it was, and how like Ruth to send it up!

"Good! Ain't it?" Mattie remarked, pleased with the evident relish with which her guest was consuming her offering.

"Best apple I ever tasted," Truxton affirmed, with spontaneous enthusiasm. "I say, Mattie, have you seen Miss Ware since that time she was here last June?"

"Yes; she was in the other day, 'n' she said it was her birthday, 'n' she wanted me to give her a birthday wish."

"And what did you wish her, Mattie?"

Truxton had set the plate aside, and was holding the child's two hands, looking into those unfathomable eyes set in the little pinched, earnest face.

"I wished her,—

> "Somethin' to have,
> Somethin' to give,
> Somethin' to love,
> An' a reason to live!"

The child had got her hands away from Truxton, as she spoke, and had folded them together so tight, in her little, intense way, that white spots came out under the pressure of the fingers.

"Who taught you that, Mattie?" and Truxton drew the little creature nearer.

"Ma learned it me, and she promised it would come true. Ma was pious. But, say!—I did n't know folks had birthdays when they got so old as that! I ain't had one since Ma died," and the child twisted herself a little, within the curve of Truxton's arm, that she might look into his face.

"Did you tell Miss Ware she was too old to have a birthday?"

"Yes; 'n' she said next time I seen you I must tell you."

"Tell me what?"

"Tell you how I'd called her old. She said you'd understand, 'cause she said you'd promised her something nice when she was old. An' she must be real old, 'cause she was grown up before, you know, 'n' now she's had a birthday. Shall you keep your promise?"

"Of course, Mattie. No one would break a promise to Miss Ware."

"Course not."

Then Mattie put up her little claw of a hand and took hold of the lapel of her visitor's coat.

"Say," she asked; "is it a present?"

"No, Mattie. I don't know of anything Miss Ware wants; do you?"

"Not ezzackly. No; I guess 'tain't presents she wants."

"Then you think there's something she wants that she has n't got?"

"I guess so; 'cause when I said my wish she said that was the nicest wish she'd ever had, 'n' she hoped it would come true."

"Say the wish again, Mattie."

And again the little hands were joined tight together, and the solemn eyes looked straight ahead, as the child repeated the lines:

"Somethin' to have,
Somethin' to give,
Somethin' to love,
An' a reason to live!"

Then Truxton repeated the words after her, and, drawing the child close again, he kissed her gently on the forehead, just as Flynn had seen Ruth do one day so long ago.

"And that's my wish for you, Mattie!" he said, as he stood up to go.

"You need n't wish 'em," she replied, in her own matter-of-fact tone, as she absently brushed her hand across the place his lips had touched. "I 've got 'em all, just like Ma promised." And already she had laid her hand on Jimmy's jacket with the evident intention of making up for lost time.

Five minutes later, when Truxton looked in again to inquire about the window-cord, which had entirely escaped his mind, he found the child bent over her work, and sweetening her labors with the remains of the apple which he had not quite finished.

Yes; little Mattie had "got 'em all!" Ruth was right when she said of their own kind, that life was more difficult to them, that there was even more suffering in it for them, and a great deal more effort. Well, it was the effort that made the suffering tolerable. It was lucky for him—and for Harkness Dole, he added, parenthetically, with a poignant recollection of Dole's strenuous face as he had passed his hand absently along the edge of that stamped-leather frame—it was well for them that they had their hands full.

And Ruth? Did Ruth really care? If he

were to be suddenly reinstated in all he had lost, just a commonplace bank-clerk, with the glamour of misfortune gone, would Ruth find it in her heart to send him messages? He had his doubts. He was almost glad not to put her to that test; or, at least, he told himself that he was! Better to be sure of her compassion, if that was the warmest feeling that he was entitled to at her hands.

Yet, somehow, the lilac-bushes, as he walked up the home path, did not look quite so dusty and dingy as they had done ten days ago. He reflected that there had been a smart rain the night before, which must have freshened them up.

And again in deference to Miss Vickery's day he lifted the brass knocker and set its echoes thundering through the halls. The brass dragon, at least, was in a good state of preservation; it was fairly likely to outlive the house, to outlive the occupants of the house.

Miss Vickery herself was looking her brightest and best, as was her wont of a Wednesday. And if this chronicle has not intruded upon her on any other day of the week than Wednesday, it has certainly evinced a discretion not other than commendable. For, surely, if our expressed preferences are not to be honored when we have attained the dignity of seventy-eight years, we might well question the advantage of living so long.

As Truxton appeared before her, hat in hand,

Miss Vickery welcomed him with her choicest Wednesday dignity.

"You are my second visitor," she remarked, with an evident humorous intention. "That is really more than I could have anticipated at this season of the year, when so few of my acquaintances have returned to town."

"And who was the other one?" Truxton inquired, as he took a seat near the little table and, picking up the cut-glass bottle of lavender water, indulged himself with a whiff of its agreeable perfume.

"I am obliged to confess that the first visit was in honor of the man of the house," she replied. "The gentleman did not give his name, but I fancy he may have been your tailor."

"My tailor? Why, that's a luxury I can hardly be said to possess, Aunt Lucretia."

"At least he brought with him a coat," the old lady explained, "which he said belonged to you, and which he was anxious to deliver into your hands. I judged that he wished to try it on. Bridget," she continued, "was quite deceived in him at first and showed him into the parlor. He was dressed like a gentleman, and persons of Bridget's class are not sufficiently discriminating to look below the surface. They do not appreciate that the rest 'is all but leather and prunella'!"

"Some mistake," Truxton declared. "I have n't been ordering any coat. The man must have got the name wrong."

"He said it was for Mr. Truxton of the Pilgrim Savings Bank. I ventured to state that you had severed your connection with that institution, but he made a most remarkable grimace, and said that the bank would hardly be such a fool as to let you go, for that you were, I think he said, 'about the best man of the gang!' His language was very singular, and I did not altogether like his use of the word 'gang.' Yet his manner was inoffensive. I concluded that he must be of foreign extraction. The country is getting quite overrun with foreigners," Miss Vickery added, with that complacent fluency which an elderly person falls into when enunciating a familiar sentiment. "One often wonders what we are coming to."

"I know that some persons feel that way, Aunt Lucretia, but there are a good many of the old stock left, and I rather guess we shall hold our own."

He had restored the cut-glass bottle to its place, and transferred his attention to the feather fan.

"Did the tailor-man have anything more to say?" he asked, opening and shutting the fan—a liberty which he would scarcely have permitted himself except under stress of anxiety. There could not be much doubt as to the identity of a visitor who looked like a gentleman and talked like a person of foreign extraction!

"He only said that he should come again this evening," Miss Vickery replied, eying the fan in so pointed a manner that Truxton hastily replaced it. Then, with interest restored to the subject in hand, she added: "He made some observation about procrastination being a thief at times, which sounded like a reminiscence of the old proverb. Altogether the man seemed an unusual and somewhat perplexing personality. Perhaps he was a tenant. I hope, Frank, that you see no reason to regret your change of plan," and the old lady looked at him through her gold-rimmed spectacles in a searching manner which was rather disconcerting to her nephew.

"No, Aunt Lucretia, I still think it was a wise step."

The subject was one to which he never voluntarily alluded. It always gave him an uncomfortable feeling of self-consciousness, a sense of double-dealing, which he hated. But he went on to say, with a fair show of spontaneity: "I am hoping to develop this tenement-house business into something really satisfactory. I don't forget your warning about being too sanguine, but—it is a kind of work I seem adapted to."

"It must have been a matter of much regret to the bank authorities," the old lady persisted, in a tone of gratified pride which betrayed the hollowness of her concern for the Pilgrim Fathers. "Mr. Ware, the son of your great-uncle John's classmate, Judge Ware, spoke extremely well of you when he was so kind as to call upon me during your absence. I was much impressed by his anxiety to obtain your address. I could only suppose that they wished to consult you about some matter of importance."

"There was a little matter that turned up while I was away," Frank admitted, though the deception went much against the grain, "that I happened to know more about than the other men."

"I almost wonder," Miss Vickery mused, "I almost wonder that, under the circumstances, you were willing to leave them on such short notice. It must have been a serious disappointment to them."

"Why, in a way, I suppose they were sorry. They have certainly been very kind about it. But there are always plenty of applicants for a comfortable berth like that, and I imagine there won't be any difficulty about filling my place."

"That may be," Miss Vickery replied, only half convinced; "but I doubt very much whether they find another man of your ability and standing. Neither the Vickerys nor the Truxtons have been in the habit of filling salaried positions of that nature," she continued, warming to her subject, "and I imagine, Frank, that in work of that kind, as well as in the higher walks of life, *blood will tell.*"

Truxton felt a creeping sensation of heat suffuse itself over face and neck.

"We must n't get conceited, Aunt Lucretia," he replied, with a forced laugh. "The men at the Pilgrim are all of good Yankee stock, and there are plenty more where they came from."

He sprang to his feet, and at that moment the click of the gate was heard at the end of the lilac walk.

"Hullo! That's Flynn, our old janitor!" he exclaimed, as he peered out into the gathering dusk. "Shall we have Bridget show him into the library, and light up?"

CHAPTER XXI.

THE TALE OF AN OLD COAT.

THE library was a square front room, on the opposite side of the hall from the long parlor. Its walls were lined with well-stocked book-shelves which had the appearance of being but rarely disturbed, while from the dim old volumes arose that delicately pervasive odor, so dear to the nostrils of the book-lover.

Truxton found Flynn standing in the middle of the room, regarding, with much interest, a bust of Socrates which showed white amid its shadowy surroundings. The light from the chandelier shone full upon the head of the latter-day sage, and brought out a curious resemblance to the deeply wrinkled physiognomy of the bust.

As Truxton entered, Flynn turned, and, indicating with an easy gesture his distinguished prototype, he remarked, "Your honorable grandfather, I suppose?" The undulatory inflection of the last open *o* conveyed such a world of wisdom and penetration that Truxton had not the heart to contradict him.

"Do you think I favor him, Flynn?" he asked, at the same time pulling forward the great leathern arm-chair which had been the property of his veritable grandfather, and motioning the old man to take a seat.

"Favor him, is it?" Flynn replied, wresting its subtle meaning from the unfamiliar phrase, and giving, the while, deliberate consideration to the youthful, clean-cut countenance before him, the lines of which were not those of abstruse speculation. "I 'm thinkin' ye 're full young to favor your grandfather!"

Then, ignoring the proffered chair, and with a sudden change from the judicial tone to one the suppressed excitement of which did not escape Truxton's notice, he said, taking the linen coat from his arm and laying it with great circumspection upon the table: "That 's the coat yez was afther wearin' the day yez was last at the counter!"

"Thanks, Flynn," said Truxton, picking up the coat, and tossing it over the back of a chair. "You were very good to bring that 'way out here. I am afraid I should have forgotten all about it until the hot weather piped up again. And now sit down and have a glass of grog. I 've got my grandfather's receipt for it—not that grandfather's,"—with a glance at the ancient bust,—"but another one's," and Truxton stepped to one of the bookcases, beneath which was a cupboard where he knew that the jovial traditions of another generation were piously embalmed in spirits.

"Naw, sorr, an' I thank ye, sorr!" Flynn protested—and then Truxton was positive that it was no light errand that had brought this unaccustomed visitor to his door.

Flynn, meanwhile, had confided his slight form, in a half-distrustful way, to the recesses of the big chair, within which he looked very small and ill at ease. "It's not a minute I'll be afther kapin' yez, sorr," he declared; "it's only the *coat* I was afther bringin' back."

"Yes, but you'll sit a while, Flynn, and tell me how things are going at the bank. Have they got the new light-shades yet? and—have they taken on anybody new?"

"Well, sorr, there's a tall, lofty young feller, wid a queer name to him altogither. Iverett James—that's him—wid his name turned wrong side before, same as the ladies' bonnets the day! An' me an' Misther Stone thinks that yoursilf forgets more over night than the new feller 'll ever know. Misther Trooxton," he continued, with a profoundly insinuating leer,—" Misther Trooxton, yez might cast an eye into the pockets of the coat there. If yez was afther puttin' annything into it, ye 'd belike have forgotten it in all the long time!"

There was no mistaking the increasing excitement of the old man's manner. He was now sitting on the extreme edge of the chair, leaning forward, the Socratic countenance gathering itself into a curious snarl of wrinkles, the small eyes twinkling sharply in the light of the gas-jets. Truxton felt himself strangely under compulsion as he stepped across the room and picked up the linen coat.

Beginning with an outside pocket, he pulled out a handkerchief, and with it came a bill, stuck fast together into a bunch. He picked up the bill, while Flynn eyed him excitedly.

"Why, what's this?" Truxton exclaimed; "I never carry money in this pocket. Flynn, what does this mean?"

"Sure, your honor'll have put a dollar bill in by mistake wid your handkerchief. If it was annything *vallible* it wad be in the *inside* pocket!"

Truxton, meanwhile, was endeavoring to unfold the bill, which adhered closely to some central object. At last it yielded its hold upon what proved to be a wad of chewing-gum, and, spreading the note out flat, Truxton read the denomination which he had already identified. The blood seemed to rush backward to his heart in an overwhelming surge. He leaned heavily against the table, his hand spread out upon the bill. When he spoke, his voice sounded to his own ears hollow and far away.

"Flynn," he said, sternly, "what do you know of this?"

And Flynn rose to his feet, with a scared and

guilty look, and, coming close up to the table, gazed through his spectacles at the bill, while gradually his face fell to an expression of abject dismay.

"Nothing, sorr; nothing at all," he protested; but there was nothing of the jaunty disclaimer with which he had once denied all knowledge of the tomato-soup, as it trickled in gory evidence from his tin pail.

"Did you put that money in that pocket?" his inquisitor demanded.

"Me!" and with a sudden jerk the old man recovered his equilibrium, and was able to enunciate, with scathing emphasis: "Me! An' is it me that would be afther *chewin' gum?*"

"Great Scott!" Truxton cried; and he sank into a chair under an overpowering conviction. "Flynn, where's Tim?" he asked.

"Tim, is it? Tim? He's to the hospital wid a broken arm; he is that!"

"How long has he been there?"

"How should I know that? Wan, two, three weeks, maybe."

Truxton was quite calm now. He had simply waked from a long nightmare. If the nightmare has been a very bad one, the blood goes a bit faster for it; that is all.

"Now, Flynn," he said, very quietly, "if you knew nothing about that money, what was the reason you were so everlastingly careful about that coat, and so particular about my looking through the pockets? There was some reason, and you may as well own up."

Then the full dignity of the pilgrim sage asserted itself. He rose to his feet, and, throwing his shoulders back, with a gesture peculiar to him in his more exalted moods, he said: "Sure, sorr, if it was mesilf, I'd not be afther lookin' for annything *valliable* in the *outside* pocket av a coat!"

There was something so impressive, so significant, in this, that Truxton found himself again under a strong compulsion to defer action, to defer thought, to defer the very emotion of deliverance, until he should have followed the unspoken behests of the old man's tone and manner.

"I don't suppose there.'s another ten-thousand-dollar gold certificate in the inside pocket," he remarked, as he turned the coat inside out, with a view to further investigation. And, lo! as he inserted his hand within the breast-pocket, his fingers closed upon a crisp piece of paper, of unmistakable texture and consistency.

A curious, creeping sensation came over him; he felt himself played upon by some insidious, abnormal agency. He did not at once pull out the money.

And Flynn, seeing his hesitancy, observing his change of countenance, seemed himself to undergo a reaction of feeling, which resulted in a sudden collapse into the embrace of the leathern chair.

Then Truxton drew forth the crisp, clean bill

that had spent the night under the blue glass vase. He scarcely needed to glance at the superscription, nor did he do more than glance at the old man's face, working visibly with conflicting emotions. Instead, he stepped to the bell-rope and, pulling it violently, he listened to an answering tintinnabulation in the remote kitchen.

"Bridget," he said, as that functionary arrived, quite breathless with curiosity, "bring me a pitcher of hot water, some glasses, a dessert-spoon, a lemon, and a knife, and,—Bridget!—bring me the sugar-bowl!"

"Now, Flynn," Truxton continued, repairing definitively to the bookcase cupboard, to which a sure instinct had guided him at the beginning of the interview; "Now, Flynn, you shall try my grandfather's receipt—unless you have a better one of your own."

Then Flynn, pulling himself together, and accepting, with evident relief, the change of subject, said: "Well, sorr, if it's a glass of grog it is,—what do you say to lavin' the limonade be?"

"What! You'd rather have it straight?"

"Well, sorr, it's not aisy to betther a good thing!"

And straight it was, and straight to the spot it went, if one might judge by the way the old man's small eyes gleamed as he took it. Or, was it not, after all, quite "straight"? Did it perhaps not lack an admixture of warmth and of sweetness, and a pleasing tartness?

For, just as the two men lifted their glasses to their lips, Truxton paused to say, with a gathering emotion in his voice : " Flynn, you are an irrational old humbug, but—here 's to the best friend a man ever had—*God bless him !* "

It was a long draught, and a strong draught, and a draught both together, and it was calculated to infuse new courage into both actors in this somewhat embarrassing situation. Yet there is no denying that Flynn, in spite of the rousing toast, in spite of the excellence of the liquor, was distinctly crestfallen at the simple and unlooked-for solution of his " protejay's " perplexities.

The toast, to be sure, had been a singularly happy and acceptable one. Far from taking umbrage at the preliminary clause, the old man found it peculiarly grateful to his feelings. The term " irrational old humbug," though not in itself flattering, had a reassuringly familiar sound to his ears, and relieved the peroration of undue and embarrassing solemnity. Just what " an irrational old humbug " might signify was a question hardly worth speculating upon, but the tone of affectionate raillery was in itself entirely satisfactory.

The cause of the old man's discomfiture was twofold. In the first place he felt that Tim, the " unhatherly young spalpeen ! " had distinctly got the better of him. He, Barney Flynn, had been thwarted in his dearest ambition by a disreputable, irresponsible little upstart. And this brings us to the real grievance.

For Flynn, in his grotesque, inarticulate fashion, really loved Truxton, and never, since little Katie died, had any aspiration been as real, as tangible to him, as this of playing the part of benignant Providence in that little affair which he had elected to adopt as the romance of his old age. If his castle in the air was built of the flimsiest, the most improbable materials, it was at least reared upon a basis of faith and affection, and its architect believed in it with all his heart.

Whether Flynn had really expected to deceive Truxton, is a question which he himself could not have answered. We all know the poignant appeal to the imagination exercised by a garment once worn by a departed friend, whether departed to a better world or to a remoter region of this questionably satisfactory one. And, as Flynn pondered, day by day, the best way of insinuating his gift into the acceptance of a beneficiary of whose willingness to take it he entertained grave doubts, he could think of no more plausible device than that of creating the fiction of the money having been, in this preposterous manner, "*mislaid*"—as he would have expressed it, with a very broad and ravelled-out emphasis on the last syllable.

Furthermore, if he had had his misgivings as to really deceiving Truxton, he perhaps entertained a sneaking hope that his "protejay" might pretend to be deceived! He was sure, at least, that he, Barney Flynn, would have made such a trifling concession as that for the sake of Katie.

Now, however, thanks to the aforesaid " young spalpeen," Flynn saw himself left quite at one side, his elaborate and careful scheme in danger of being shelved entirely, himself of being treated as a side issue. And, although he drained his glass of excellent liquor with becoming spirit, and although he accepted, graciously, the handsome tribute of the toast, his chagrin was profound.

Truxton, on his part, was as prompt to perceive the old man's discomfiture as he had been quick to take in the bald facts of the situation. And scarcely had he drained his glass—the contents of which he had taken the precaution to weaken largely, being himself unhabituated to such powerful potations—than he was visited by one of those inspirations which have their source in something deeper and finer than mere quickness of wit. As he set his glass upon the table he said, in a tone of conviction: " Flynn, I had no idea you were such a capitalist! If I had known that, there's nobody I should have sooner asked to help me out of this scrape ! "

" An' a proud day it wad ha' been for mesilf, your honor ! " Flynn replied, with a gleam of returning animation ; " a grand day indade ! "

And Truxton, fearing that his statement was too preposterous for credence, made haste to add: " Of course I should have given you proper securities. The fact is, Flynn, I am something of a capitalist myself. It is really I that own that block you live in. I did n't want to brag, so I only told you that I had charge of it."

The old familiar look of unfathomable wisdom diffused itself over the Socratic countenance, and, with a shrug of the shoulders, Flynn remarked, "An' did yez suppose I did n't know that?"

Then, leaning forward, and gazing up at Truxton with the most ingratiating leer, he added: "Sure, sorr, there 's other tinimints as wad be betther for a taste of dacency and Christianity, an' if a bit o' money like that—" a change in Truxton's countenance turned the tenor of his argument, and he finished, rather lamely: "It 's a good *invistmint* I 'd be glad to get!"

"There are lots of good investments, Flynn," Truxton replied, hastily. "You had better talk with Mr. Smith about it."

"Wid Misther Smith?" and the old man's voice was overspread with cold disgust. "Wid Misther Smith? An' what for should I be afther talkin' wid Misther Smith?"

"Well, only that he has had a good deal of experience, and I think he would be willing to advise you."

"An' it 's not advice I 'm wantin' at all! It 's an *invistmint!* An' if your honor 'll be afther *invistin*' the bit o' money there, it 's a proud day it 'll be for the ould man. It 's not the interist I 'm afther," he added, with unmistakable intention; "it 's an *invistmint!* An' if your honor 'll put it in your own name, it's aisy I 'll be, an' well I 'll slape!"

The excitement had returned upon the old fellow, and Truxton thought it well to humor him—so far at least as to retain the custody of the money for the night. He wondered whether the toast could have gone to the hard old head. But, no! The visitor's step was steady when he rose to go, and his speech was quite coherent.

If there had been any doubt as to Flynn's condition being entirely normal, it would have been dispelled by the studied nonchalance with which he remarked, when on the point of departure: "Hersilf was in at the bank wan day, wid a big hat on her. Aw, but it's spry she is on her feet!"

And so naturally did the information fall in with the steady undercurrent of his thoughts that Truxton, far from resenting it, replied, audaciously, "You ought to see that young lady paddle a canoe, Flynn!"

Now, Flynn knew nothing of canoes, and less of paddles, but the manner of the statement implied a confidence that he knew how to value. He did not reply directly, but, glancing up at the shadowy old mansion, only faintly illuminated by a distant street-lamp, he remarked: "It's a foine risidince yez have here, sorr;—fit for *anny lady in the land!*"—with which delicate insinuation, the quaint old figure, in its black coat and silk hat, made a dignified exit at the front gate.

Then Truxton, still standing on the lower step, whence he had so acceptably sped his parting guest, glanced up at the old house. Through the window of the library he could see the bust of Socrates gleaming white, yet incalculably ancient, above the rows of time-worn volumes; the parlor at the right of the door had not been lighted. Aunt Lucretia had doubtless fallen asleep after the uneventful day for which she had so punctiliously prepared herself. The rest of the house, too, was wrapped in darkness; like the shades of the past, it hung closely, almost obliteratingly, about the sturdy old walls.

A sudden pity clutched the young man's heart; pity for the men of yesterday, whose story is told, pity for the old house that would not long be a home, pity for the lonely old woman whose youth was gone, pity for all who were not, like himself, at the beginning of all things: the beginning of ambition, the beginning of achievement, the beginning of something else which he would not name, but which brought his mind back, with a strong impulse of tenderness, to the old man who never forgot "how spry she was on her feet!"

CHAPTER XXII.

THE PROSE OF IT.

IT was close upon quarter-day, and the bank was thronged with depositors. Every man of the force was hard at work, from Rathbone, whose receipts for the day were forging along toward seventy thousand dollars, down to Beardsley, the "aisy-goin'," who handled small slips of white paper, whereon were inscribed mystic letters and figures, with an intensity of concentration which left no room for criticism even in the mind of Flynn, his outspoken detractor. Little Billy Denison was obliged to keep his risibles in check in the very face of Bridget Ballahak, who had grown if possible more demonstrative than ever since last she routed him; while Polly Voo was forced to confine his remarks to the tersest English. Aleck Plummer, who possessed the art of carrying on several trains of thought at once, doubtless indulged in many a mental note upon the salient points of the situation, but he refrained from embarrassing the labored calculations of George Bodley with an untimely enunciation of them.

Flynn was in his glory, marshalling his flock of vaguely wandering capitalists with a consistent firmness that could only have been acquired by long practice. Yet, to the close observer, had any one commanded the leisure for enacting that always remunerative part, a certain added haughtiness would have been discernible in the old man, an ineffable air of superiority, the misleading outward sign of an inward exultation. And, if there was no opportunity on the other side of the counter for the expression of kindred emotions, it is nevertheless true that there was not a man in the gang whose heart was not lighter, whose spirits were not higher than they had been for many a long day.

The ugly mystery which had hung over them like a pall, which had cast its shadow upon all concerned, which had seemed to encompass the bank itself in its sinister folds—that mystery was dispelled, and once more the seventy-five years' record of the noble old Pilgrim stood out clear and unimpeachable.

Even the front office shared something of the exhilaration of the moment, for Joseph Rand, the chief clerk, had reported, after hours the preceding day, that Mr. Edwin Coleridge, the president of the bank, had made a joke; a thing which had not occurred before within the memory of man. The joke was an old one, and one which hardly had the stamina for hard usage, yet, falling from the unaccustomed lips of the president, it had become invested with an importance not its own, and, being promptly embalmed in the minds of all who heard, it was insured an undeserved longevity.

A report was furthermore current to the effect that Mr. Smith had gone so far as to say that, if he had been mistaken in Frank Truxton, he should never have trusted his own judgment again; a circumstance which would have caused a serious revolution in Mr. Smith's methods, and a general reversal of his mental processes. For the vice-treasurer was a student of character, and he justly considered as final his conclusions on that head.

As the big doors closed behind the last depositor, Flynn sauntered up the floor, wrapped in the approval of a good conscience. Andy Stone, who had burst into uncontrollable melody, was singing:

> "Beat the trumpet, blow the drum,
> Quarter-day has almost come!"

And although the sentiment in itself had no immediate bearing on the situation, the triumphant strain was regarded by all as a fit expression of the dominant emotion.

"Hullo, Flynn!" Polly Voo called, with a patronizing condescension which left Flynn as unaffected as water leaves a duck's back; "perhaps you would like to know that your *protejay* has come out of his devil of a scrape with no bones broken."

"Has he, indade?" Flynn replied, not staying his step, but passing, with an air of superb indifference, into the back office. "Has he, indade?" he repeated, in a low, ecstatic guttural, as he pulled on his overcoat, and passed a handkerchief affectionately around the glistening crown of his silk hat. "Has he, indade?"

For Truxton had not betrayed the secret of Flynn's ill-starred financial stroke in his behalf. There was not a man in the bank to whom he would have ventured to confide such a weapon as that against his old friend. And it was with scarcely less loyalty, though by different means, that he had undertaken to shield the young apprentice in crime who had so incontinently fallen a victim to his own better instincts.

Truxton's first act, on the morning after the return of the linen coat laden with such preposterous revelations, was to visit Tim, where he lay, chafing and fretting, in the hospital ward. The lad's exuberant capers on the treacherous floor of the floating pier had resulted in a compound fracture of a serious nature, and the tedious confinement it entailed would have been a sufficiently severe trial to an active boy, had his conscience been never so free of reproach. To Tim, the days and weeks of suspense had been a period of real agony of mind, and the sudden apparition of Frank Truxton, pregnant as it was with distressing possibilities, was nothing short of a relief to him.

The interview was a long one, and before it ended Truxton knew that not a fibre of the boy's consciousness but had been laid bare to him. As he rose to go, he took in his own the bony left hand, so unnaturally, so pathetically clean, and said, heartily: "Then, Tim, that's a bargain. I'm to do what I can to get the bank to let you off, and when we've set you on your feet, you're going to walk straight!"

"I guess that's so, sir!" Tim answered; and if there was anything wanting to the verbal expression of his sentiments, the vigorous blinking of his eyes against an importunate moisture, and the intense, clinging grip of the bony hand, were indicative of a degree of emotion which augured well for his sincerity.

And even after that, and even after a memorable half-hour spent in the front office of the bank, Truxton did not take any immediate steps to come again into touch with Ruth. He had a curious shrinking from doing so. He knew he could not see her, he doubted whether he could force himself to write to her, without making that direct appeal in which he felt he was not yet justified. Truxton was far from sharing Flynn's opinion that what he wanted he must have. On the contrary, he believed more profoundly than ever that what he wanted he must earn. And if it had suddenly been demonstrated that his record was clean, he still felt that it presented very little to brag of.

"Yes," he said to Harkness Dole, in response to the congratulations of the latter, the day after what Harvey Winch called the *daynoumong;* " it seems it was a blunder instead of a crime. Opinions vary as to which of the two is less discreditable to the person concerned."

"I presume the bank is clear on that head. They are ready to take you on again, it seems?"

"They profess to be; but I don't really suppose they think any better of a man for letting ten thousand dollars slip through his fingers. No, Dole; I have n't covered myself with glory, and I don't propose to embarrass them by taking advantage of their indulgence. I shall go back tomorrow, and lend a hand over the October flurry, and until they 've worked in their new man, and then I shall quit. It 's not much of a sacrifice, either," he added; "for I believe I have got a fairly good thing here." And he looked about the shabby little den where they were sitting, with an undisguised pride of ownership that struck his companion as indication of the " stuff " that was in him.

It was the first time the two men had met since the Sunday evening when Dole had suffered signal defeat in his effort to straighten things out. He had respected Truxton's very evident wish to be left alone, and he had persuaded the demonstrative Shepleigh to do the same, after the latter, also, had been baffled in his attempt at intervention. Now, however, things were changed, and no sooner had he learned that this was the case than he made haste to look Truxton up.

He found him hard at work in his new office, and although the room was small and dim and scantily furnished, it had already taken on that air of respectability which emanates from a desk, a swivel-chair, a city directory, and a clerkly ledger. There were no shades in the two windows, which opened upon a paved courtyard, but the panes were clean, and invited the little light there was. A map of the city hung opposite the window, and, in a shadowy corner, Dole espied a paddle standing, blade upwards, against the wall. On the desk near the inkstand lay a piece of common evergreen. It was all like an open book to Dole.

"You've got a snug little hole here," he remarked; "but you'll need larger quarters before long."

"I hardly think so," Truxton rejoined. "A hanging book-shelf and a good safe is all I need for the present, and there's plenty of room for that."

Dole hesitated a moment. He had been routed once by this young fellow with the youthful, inexperienced face—less inexperienced, now, however, than it had been. There were no new lines that he could discover, but it struck him that the whole expression of the face was somehow less pliant; that there was a new significance in the look of the eyes, always alert, but now grown intent. He should not, to-day, have questioned the existence of nerve in the possessor of this countenance; he should have credited him at once with a sure aim, whatever weapon he might elect to use.

Dole was smoking, as a man will when he wishes to seem more at his ease than he is. Truxton was conscious of no such necessity. There had been no appreciable pause in the talk, for these observations, which take time when reduced to words, had been merely a matter of total impression in Dole's mind.

"I may as well tell you," he was saying, "that I am the party who has been negotiating for that property of yours."

"I knew it," said Truxton, composedly; "either you or Shepleigh."

"How did you know?"

"Because things were going so smoothly."

"I did not offer more than it was worth."

"No; but you did not offer less; so of course I knew."

"Nevertheless, from a business point of view I am disappointed not to get it."

"Very likely," Truxton assented, with frank scepticism; "only yours did not happen to be the business point of view."

"Not when I went into it, I grant you. But I have looked things over pretty carefully since then, and I think it a good investment."

"Do you still want it?"

"As an investment, I should be glad of it; but —I shall not take it."

There was a pause, during which Truxton absently turned the leaves of the directory. Dole, perceiving that he had something to say, waited for him to speak.

"See here, Dole," Truxton said, at last; "is that money of yours still going begging?"

"Yes."

"Why could n't we——"

"Exactly!" Dole cut in. "That is what I was coming at. The fact is," and he settled back, as comfortably as might be, in his wooden chair; "the fact is, I 've had something of the sort in mind for years, but I have n't known where to turn for a manager."

"There are several pieces of property in this vicinity that are going down hill. It 's a good centre."

"And you think we could make a purchase?"

"It 's my opinion that we could. The thing has n't paid so well, lately, because the decent class of tenants fight shy of these rattle-traps. But the locality has its advantages, and if we could lump things a little we could work up a feature or two that would draw. What I should aim for in the end "—and Truxton leaned forward, warming to his subject—" would be pretty much all the block,—four sides of it,—with a big playground for the kids and a fountain in the middle.

Tell you what, Dole, a fountain would be money in our pockets!"

A contemplative puff of blue rings issued from between Dole's lips, before he said: "I suppose if we got a good start we could kind of *crowd the others out; eh?*"

"That's the idea! And when we were once on our legs, we could make our payments in stock —if we wanted to."

"Have you talked with anyone about this?"

"Yes; with Bowdoin J. Wheeler. He was sceptical at first; it's his business to be. He was afraid it smacked of philanthropy. But I dwelt upon the sordid gains, and he's caving— gradually. He has been playing into my hands lately. He has given me two permanent jobs."

"Do you expect him to take a hand in the scheme?"

"Can't tell; he's one of these cautious chaps. You never know which way they'll jump. But I've got a five years' lease on this property of his, and I rather expect to haul it in and him with it, before we are through."

Later, after some further discussion of available properties: "How much do you think you could handle?" Dole asked.

"More than we could get hold of; and of course the sooner we need a clerk the better."

"I rather think we should expand pretty fast. I'm ready to go in to the amount of something considerable, myself, and I know one or two men who might like it. I don't think we shall have any lack of capital. And, by the way, Truxton, you must stick out for your commission. Don't listen to any talk of salary."

"A salary! I should think not! Just you wait and see if I don't carry things with a high hand! But, seriously, Dole; we'll get matters arranged to suit ourselves before we let anyone else in; won't we?"

"I fancy we can manage to keep control of things," Dole opined, with a comfortable assurance. "Have you anybody in mind to come in with us?"

"Well, yes; I have;" and Truxton picked up the bit of evergreen and, lifting it to his face, drew in the lingering fragrance with a deep breath.

Dole, who fancied that he could guess the direction his companion's thoughts had taken, was far afield in his surmise. And even had the gift of second sight been his, to the extent of showing him the secluded eyrie of the pilgrim sage,—carpet-covered sofa, Turkey-red hangings, blue glass vase and all,—he could hardly have divined its many-sided associations in Truxton's mind.

"And who is it?" he inquired, rather reluctantly, for he had an impression that he must seem very obtuse to pursue the mater-of-fact theme of their discourse.

"Do you suppose," and Truxton laid down the bit of evergreen, but not before his thoughts had veered in the direction Dole had already imputed to them,—" do you suppose the concern is safe enough for us to let in our old janitor? He has set his heart upon some sort of partnership with me." And thereupon Truxton told the tale of the linen coat, and with none the less relish for the abstemiousness he had hitherto observed on the subject.

Dole listened, half incredulous, cudgelling his brain for some explanation, other than the obvious one, of such a phenomenal exhibition of magnanimity. It was something too contrary to his experience to be accounted for in terms of every-day philosophy.

"What did you say to him?" he asked, regarding Truxton with open curiosity.

"I believe I first called him names, and then I told him that if I had known he was such a capitalist, I should have applied to him before."

"Which was not strictly veracious."

"No; only civilized!" and, with a flash of reminiscence, both men recalled the occasion of their first meeting, the candles and the flowers and the light talk of that dinner, and both, presumably, thought of Ruth.

"You have the gift, Truxton," Dole remarked, sighing heavily. He had not done such a thing in public before since he was grown up. Yet the tone was a cheerful one in which he continued: "You 're evidently the man to deal with the paddy-whacks,—to say nothing of the rest of us!"

"And you think we might let Flynn in?" Truxton persisted, still very much in earnest. "We could give him extra securities, I suppose?"

"Yes; we'll make it as good as governments —and at six per cent! The old chap cast his bread upon the waters, that time, with a vengeance!"

"I suppose he did; but, do you know, Dole," and Truxton picked up the bit of evergreen once more, and once more he lifted it, absently, to his face, "I can't get it out of my head that Flynn has somehow been the arbiter of my destinies! When he cocks his head on one side and patronizes me, I can't, for the life of me, keep from feeling that my fate is in his hands!"

"Flynn is your creation, Truxton," Dole rejoined; "and I don't know that you could be in better hands."

"My creation? How do you make that out?"

"It is very easily demonstrated. You certainly can't deny that your Flynn is a totally different person from anybody's else Flynn. And whatever it is in you that has called him out, it is a kind of fate that will *see you through!*"

This somewhat oracular statement was delivered with such unaccustomed warmth of conviction, that Truxton, dropping his bit of evergreen, laughed outright.

"Look here, Dole," he cried, "is it my vote you're after?"

"No, Truxton," and the answer was given

with a calm disregard of his companion's irreverent mirth; "no; what I hope for, as you very well know, is a chance to cast my vote for you, one of these days."

Then Truxton, in his turn grown suddenly serious, said: "There's no telling what may happen—one of these days. That is what makes life so tremendously worth while!"

"You find life worth while, then?"

"I do, indeed; don't you?"

Dole hesitated, looking across at the strong, hopeful young face he liked so well; and then he answered, quietly:

"Once in a great while, perhaps—*by proxy!*"

CHAPTER XXIII.

THE POETRY OF IT.

ONE glorious October day Frank Truxton came striding along that humble thoroughfare which lends its name to Miss Vickery's Broad Street block, whistling like a mocking-bird. If the tune of the *Lumberman's Ditty* was lending itself with surprising elasticity to a simple theme quite unrelated to it in rhythm and metre; if the strictly trochaic refrain: "Ruth is coming home to-day," had no quarrel with the anapæstic swing of the melody adapted more particularly to:

"Give a shanty boy rum and there's nothing goes wrong!"

this was perhaps due to the broadly harmonizing mood of the performer's mind.

Ruth was coming home to-day—so much he had learned from Caleb—and this very evening he should be with her in the pleasant old house in the elm-grown square. He should look into her face, he should hear her voice, he should touch her hand; and at last, at last, he should be free to follow the promptings of the moment. He did not try to foretell what they would be; he was content to trust himself to them. Enough, that Ruth was coming home to-day!

To whistle in tune is a less usual accomplishment than is generally believed, and it lends an individuality to the note which may be recognized even by those who are incapable of defining it. The Widow O'Toole, for instance, was wont to rise hastily to her feet, the moment that particular sound struck her ear, and to take agitated counsel with her looking-glass before responding to the rap which was sure to follow.

To-day, however, that excellent tenant had stepped upstairs an hour since, just to show a neighborly interest in the new tooth appertaining to the Talligan baby, and so animated was the conversation with the baby's mother, to the delights of which she had succumbed, and so spiritedly was it carried on by both ladies at once, that the cheerful whistle quite escaped the widow's notice.

Yet the pleasant tenement on the ground floor was not deserted, nor was that familiar strain lost upon the temporary occupant of the O'Toole rocker. Ruth Ware, sitting, lost in thought, at the sunny kitchen window behind the geraniums, experienced a sudden sense as of the breath of balsam and the sound of crackling birch-wood. The color flew to her cheek, and she sprang to her feet and stood, with 'bated breath, waiting. She did not answer the short, sharp rap that came at the door. It was *himsilf*, and he would enter as he had done on that day when they had first met and talked together.

Then Truxton turned the handle, noticing, with the quickness bred of habit, that it was getting a bit loose in the socket, and, as he closed the door behind him, he glanced through into the kitchen. There, in a wide shaft of sunshine, stood a figure clad in a dark-green gown, the warm, soft coil of hair showing beneath the dark felt hat, just as it had done so many months ago, and stirring in Truxton a reminiscence of the way the September sunshine had lighted up the deep green of the pine-woods only yesterday !

He did not pause to notice whether the mistress of the establishment was present, he did not yet take in the miracle of her absence. With eyes and thoughts for nothing but the girl he loved, the girl he had almost lost, the girl he must win now, to-day, this very hour, he crossed the intervening space, and his two hands clasped both of Ruth's in a strong, firm clasp, as masterful and as tender as the power which drew them together.

And neither Ruth nor Truxton thought to say a word at the very first ; and although the moment of silence was but a moment, it seemed to each an incalculable space of time, a time of clearest vision, of profoundest understanding.

Ruth was the first to recover her self-possession.

Withdrawing her hands gently, and not in the least as if she were denying him anything, she said, with a curious little catch of feeling in her voice : " We shall have to get Margaret to introduce us all over again,—the time has been so long ! "

" Long ! " said Truxton ; " it has been a lifetime ! Yes," with a conviction half jest, half earnest, " I am sure it has been a lifetime, and that, of course, makes us old folks ! And so the time has come for me to tell you—what was it that I was going to tell you ? "

" Something very foolish, I am sure, for you were in a very foolish frame of mind when you wrote that miserable little note."

" Foolish ? " he repeated. " Foolish ? Do you think so ? "

" Of course I think so, but—I am glad you wrote it."

" Why ? "

" Because—" she hesitated, and, turning toward the window, she pressed a geranium leaf between her fingers to wake the sleeping fragrance. " Because—*it was like you.*"

He came and stood beside her. He could not see her face now—it was hidden by the rim of her hat, as she bent over the flowers,—but he could divine the look in it.

" If it was like me to be foolish then," he answered, gently, " I am grown very wise now ; too wise to mistake the true relation of things again."

And Ruth stood very still, looking out into the sunny yard, where a desultory blue apron on the clothes-line rose and fell with the stirring of a light breeze.

"I should not again be deterred by any external thing from seeking—" he paused an instant—"from seeking the best gifts."

Then Ruth, with an instinctive impulse to defer the utterance of that word which was too precious to be hastened, too sure of being spoken to be jeopardized by delay, said, quietly: "I think you have been seeking the best gifts ever since I have known you. And now Harkness Dole has told me that you have the means of doing so much, so much!"

"Yes," Truxton answered, accepting the momentary swerving from his theme which she had decreed, "yes; and apart from its being a means of livelihood, it is the work I care most for—to help very poor people to decent homes. I am sure it means a great deal to them."

"I am sure of it," said Ruth. "It has been the dream of my life to do that, or at least to see it done. There is so little that a woman can really do."

"And yet," said Truxton, gravely, "we all know that without a woman there can never be a home. Ruth," and his voice dropped to a low tone of passionate entreaty, "Ruth, am I to have a home—one of these days? At your hands, Ruth?"

And it was Ruth's face—not her lips—Ruth's face, that "thought of God," that answered him, as she placed her hand in his.

Then a canary-bird over the way burst into the most ecstatic strain, and the blue apron in the yard began a dance of joy, and the scarlet geranium fairly gleamed in the sunshine, and, under cover of all that joyous rioting, Ruth and Truxton entered into Paradise.

And presently—was it a moment later? was it an hour?—the Widow O'Toole appeared, breathless but voluble. She had not been five minutes away an' it was Mr. Talligan as had got a job on the electrics an' Mrs. Talligan that proud you 'd ha' thought her man was the Prisidint himsilf an' she, Mrs. O'Toole, had seen the Prisidint wid her own eyes whin she was a gyurl an' beggin' your pardon the possessor of a nate figger of her own an' what was the Prisidint but a man in coat an' pants like anny other man? An' a foine thing it was to have a man on the electrics an' his pay comin' in reg'lar bad times an' good times an' the childer growin' up an' Dinnis sellin' papers wid a voice on him as wad make your blood run cowld wid his murdhers an' explosions an' railroad accidints!

And Ruth and Truxton, being in Paradise, found the voluble widow as interesting and exhilarating a companion as an angel with wings.

Would Margaret come and work for Mrs. Ware a few days and help them get the house to rights for the winter ? She would that ! An' she had tould Mrs. Talligan only yisterday, no, it was Monday whin they was both hangin' out the wash an' they always done it peaceable an' no words between 'em like the Widow Dolan an' Kate McCoy that niver could stand in the same yard an' not fight she 'd work her fingers to the bone for Mrs. Ware anny day in the week for the sake of Miss Ruth an' the swate eyes of her. An' it was the nixt marnin' she was wanted ? The nixt marnin' she wad come ready to turn her hand to annything Miss Ruth's honorable mother might require. An' was it two dollars Misther Trooxton was wantin' ? An' if it was two hunderd he should have it for there was nothing she wad refuse to himsilf as himsilf was always so accommodatin'!

Now Mrs. O'Toole, with all her natural gift of eloquence, was not often betrayed into such extravagant hyperbole as this. She was clearly under the stimulus of some unusual excitement, and both her guests fell to speculating as to what it might be. They were destined to discover that, with all their pride in her acquaintance, they had not yet fathomed the O'Toole. On the contrary, it was the O'Toole who had fathomed them !

Was it because they took so naturally to one another's society ? Was it because they were so manifestly destined for one another ? Was it because of a certain look on their faces which her torrent of eloquence had failed to dispel ?

As she opened the door for their simultaneous departure, she exclaimed, with a pious impetuosity not to be restrained, nor yet to be misunderstood: "The saints save ye—*the twos of ye!*"—and then, with a sudden change of tone from the spiritual to the mundane, she called after them: "An' niver forget that it was the Widow O'Toole as made yez acquainted!"

When they had beaten a hasty retreat, Truxton, with a joyous laugh that scorned the thought of discomfiture, said: "Since blessings are in order, Ruth, what do you say to coming to see Aunt Lucretia? It's only fifteen minutes' walk, and—it's her day," he added, with a humorous appreciation of the general fitness of things.

And Ruth, as joyful as he, and as spontaneous, accepted.

"For, to tell the truth,"—she said, with a little buoyant thrill in her voice, as if she were so happy that she could afford to make game of herself,—"to tell you the truth, I have longed to know Miss Vickery, ever since Margaret described her, 'wid the red scarf around hersilf.' And since you would not make it easy for me, you have forced me to extreme measures."

If only Flynn could have seen Ruth's dancing eyes, if only he could have heard the daring challenge of Truxton's voice, as he retorted: "Then I am to understand that it is solely to Aunt Lucretia that I owe a certain gratifying admission that you made to me, a few minutes ago?"

"To Aunt Lucretia, yes," she said; "and——"

"And——?"

"And—to *himsilf!*"

THE END.

www.ingramcontent.com/pod-product-compliance
Lightning Source LLC
Chambersburg PA
CBHW031858220426
43663CB00006B/678